Securing Africa's Land for Shared Prosperity

Sub-Saharan Africa

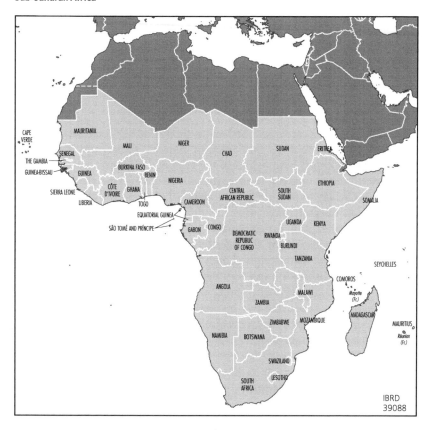

CAPE VERDE

MAURITANIA

SENEGAL

THE GAMBIA

GUINEA-BISSAU

GUINEA

SIERRA LEONE

LIBERIA

CÔTE D'IVOIRE

BURKINA FASO

MALI

GHANA

TOGO

BENIN

NIGER

NIGERIA

CAMEROON

EQUATORIAL GUINEA

SÃO TOMÉ AND PRÍNCIPE

GABON

CONGO

CHAD

CENTRAL AFRICAN REPUBLIC

DEMOCRATIC REPUBLIC OF CONGO

SUDAN

SOUTH SUDAN

UGANDA

RWANDA

BURUNDI

TANZANIA

ERITREA

ETHIOPIA

SOMALIA

KENYA

ANGOLA

ZAMBIA

NAMIBIA

BOTSWANA

ZIMBABWE

MOZAMBIQUE

MALAWI

COMOROS

Mayotte (Fr.)

MADAGASCAR

SEYCHELLES

MAURITIUS

Réunion (Fr.)

SWAZILAND

SOUTH AFRICA

LESOTHO

IBRD
39088

Titles in the Africa Development Forum Series

All books in the Africa Development Forum series are available for free at
https://openknowledge.worldbank.org/handle/10986/2150

Contents

Figure

Tables

Foreword

Few development challenges in Africa are as pressing and controversial as land ownership and its persistent gap between rich and poor communities.

With a profound demographic shift in Africa from rural areas to the cities where half of all Africans will live by 2050, these gaps will become steadily more pronounced as governments and communities rise to the challenge of growing enough affordable nutritious food for all families to thrive on the continent.

In some countries in the region, these gaps—allied as they are with high poverty rates and large-scale unemployment—have become sufficiently wide to undermine shared growth and social cohesion.

Women are especially vulnerable. They make up 70 percent of Africa's farmers and yet, for the most part, are locked out of land ownership by customary laws. Without a title to the land they farm, women are unable to raise the money needed to improve their small harvests or to raise living standards. This injurious legacy perpetuates poverty and blights the lives of women who are the backbone of Africa's farming, present and future.

Many countries around the world have grappled with the challenge of landlessness and inequality of land ownership. However, in Africa, which has 202 million hectares or half the world's total holdings of useable uncultivated fertile land, it is accentuated by extremely low agricultural productivity—only 25 percent of potential. Despite this abundant land and mineral wealth, much of Africa remains poor and too few countries have been able to translate their rapid economic growth into significantly less poverty and more opportunity. As this timely new report demonstrates persuasively, poor land governance—the system that determines and administers land rights—may be the root of this grievous problem. The vast majority of African countries are using land administration systems they inherited at independence, along with survey and mapping techniques that are antiquated.

Not surprisingly, only 10 percent of Africa's rural land is registered. The remaining 90 percent is undocumented and informally administered, which makes it susceptible to land grabbing, expropriation without fair compensation,

Abbreviations

ADR	alternative dispute resolution
AFD	Agence Française de Développement
AfDB	African Development Bank
AFREF	African geodetic reference frame
AU	African Union
CORS	continuously operating reference station
CRO	certificate of rights of occupancy
FAO	Food and Agriculture Organization of the United Nations
FLOSS	free/libre/open-source software
FOSS	free open-source software, also known as F/OSS
GIS	geographic information system
GNSS	global navigational satellite system
GPS	global positioning system
GRF	geodetic reference frame
LIS	land information system
LPI	Land Policy Initiative
LSBM	large-scale base mapping
NSDI	national spatial data infrastructure
OECD	Organisation for Economic Co-operation and Development
PFRs	*plan foncier ruraux* (rural land use plans)
SDI	spatial data infrastructure
WGS-84	World Geodetic System 1984
WSWB	willing-seller willing-buyer

they have made a commitment, through a declaration adopted by the African Union Heads of State and Government summit in July 2009 in Libya, to develop and implement comprehensive land policies, guided by the African Union's *Framework and Guidelines on Land Policy in Africa* (African Union, African Development Bank, and UN Economic Commission for Africa 2009).

The Challenge

Despite the determination and effort of leaders to improve land governance, many challenges exist. The following are the most binding:

- *Land grabs.* Investors have claimed millions of hectares (at least 1 million each in Ethiopia, Liberia, Mozambique, and Sudan between 2004 and 2009), and poor governance leads to violations of the principles for responsible agro-investment and dispossession of local communities (Deininger et al. 2011; Cotula et al. 2009).
- *Land vulnerability.* Only about 10 percent of rural land in Sub-Saharan Africa is registered; the rest is undocumented, informally administered, and thus vulnerable to land grabbing and expropriation without adequate compensation, especially for women, who are often further disadvantaged by cultural practices.
- *Inefficient land administration.* It takes twice as long and costs twice as much to transfer land in Sub-Saharan Africa as in Organisation for Economic Co-operation and Development (OECD) countries (World Bank 2012b).
- *Corruption.* According to a study in 61 countries by the Food and Agriculture Organization (FAO) and Transparency International, weak governance increases the likelihood of corruption in land administration (Arial, Fagan, and Zimmermann 2011).
- *Low capacity and demand for professionals.* Ghana, Kenya, and Uganda each have fewer than 10 professional land surveyors per 1 million population versus Malaysia (197) and Sri Lanka (150). Even these are underemployed: of Kenya's 206 registered land surveyors, only 85 are practicing. Building capacity without making complementary investments in land administration will be futile.

The Opportunities

The challenges are great and require enormous effort compared to past efforts, which were modest and limited to policy and piloting. Nevertheless, the opportunities for scaling up have never been better:

- *Higher returns.* Surging commodity prices and foreign direct investment (potentially increasing agricultural yields and markets) increase the potential return on investment in land administration.

- *Sustainable investment.* Increased investment in agriculture adds pressure but also creates opportunities to document land rights and reduce the risk of dispossessing local communities while ensuring investment deals.

- *Regional and global initiatives for land reform.* The African Union's land policy framework is in place, and a Five-Year Strategic Plan (2012–16) to implement it is being finalized. Other initiatives include the *Principles for Responsible Agro-Investment* and the FAO-led *Voluntary Guidelines on Responsible Governance of Tenure of Land.*

- *Basic land laws.* As of 2002, at least 20 countries in Sub-Saharan Africa recognized customary land rights and gender equality (Deininger 2003), and many others in the region have since followed suit.

- *Lower costs and greater efficiency.* New technologies (such as satellites) have the potential to reduce the cost of land administration (by replacing aerial photomaps costing US$150 per square kilometer with Google Earth, which is free, and satellite imagery costing US$25 per square kilometer), and at least 26 countries in Sub-Saharan Africa are replacing their geodetic infrastructure with low-cost global positioning systems for conducting uniform, cost-effective surveys. At least 15 countries in the region have ongoing initiatives to computerize their land registries, improving efficiency and reducing costs and corruption.

In addition, many countries have piloted fast, effective, and low-cost approaches to access, register, and administer land rights:

- *Registering communal lands quickly and cost-effectively.* Tanzania has surveyed almost all of its communal lands; about 60 percent have been registered, at an average cost of about US$500 per village. Ghana and Mozambique are poised to scale up their communal land registration pilots. Mexico's successful registration of communal lands (*ejidos*) during the 1990s offers positive lessons for these countries.

- *Registering individual land rights quickly and inexpensively without using a base map.* In 2003–05, Ethiopia issued certificates for 20 million parcels of land at less than US$1 per parcel (with positive impacts on investment and gender equity) and is piloting a cadastral index map that costs less than US$5 per parcel; its total cost of registration is well below that in comparable countries (US$20 per parcel). Vietnam used a similar model in the 1990s to issue many land use certificates at low cost, but did not map the land.

- *Registering individual land rights quickly and inexpensively using a base map.* In June 2012 Rwanda completed a nationwide program to issue land titles (with a photomap) at about US$10 per parcel, with significant positive impacts on investment and gender equity. Madagascar, Namibia, and

Tanzania have piloted a similar approach, which is also similar to Thailand's successful 20-year Land Titling Program but is faster and less expensive, as the spatial framework is based entirely on a photomap.

- *Registering communal and individual rights together.* Benin, Burkina Faso, and Côte d'Ivoire have piloted cost-effective and participatory rural land tenure maps to register individual and communal lands; further refinements are planned with a view to scaling up.

- *Modernizing land administration services for efficiency and transparency.* Ghana reduced the number of days to transfer property from 169 in 2005 to 34 in 2011 and increased land-related revenue from US$12 million in 2003 to US$132 million in 2010 by decentralizing and computerizing its land registries, merging its land agencies, and strengthening property valuation. Uganda is about to complete a successful pilot that computerized land records and registration systems, reducing the number of days to transfer property from 227 in 2007 to 48 in 2011.

- *Redistributing land for shared growth and poverty reduction.* Following Brazil's successful model of market-assisted land reform, Malawi successfully piloted a community-based willing-seller willing-buyer approach to land reform, benefiting more than 15,000 poor farm families, raising agricultural incomes by 40 percent a year, and attaining an economic internal rate of return of 20 percent. South Africa has been less successful, redistributing to black farmers only 7.2 percent of land owned by white farmers since 1994 and having only a minimal impact on beneficiaries' livelihoods.

- *Regularizing land tenure for squatters in urban slums.* Learning from experiences in East Asia and Latin America, Kenya, Lesotho, and Tanzania are developing and piloting efficient approaches that rely on bulk surveying and land use planning to regularize land tenure in urban slums.

The Key to Leveraging Land for Development: Scaling Up Reforms and Investments

For countries to boost governance, improved approaches and comprehensive policy reforms will need to be scaled up across the continent. This book suggests building a scaling-up program with 10 elements. The program is intended to step up comprehensive policy reforms and investments in land administration and to accelerate shared and sustained growth for poverty reduction. The program is estimated to cost US$4.5 billion over 10 years (see table O.1). The details, including costs, benefits, and implementation, are discussed in the sections that follow.

Table O.1 Key Elements of and Pathways to Scaling Up Land Administration in Sub-Saharan Africa

Key element	Cost estimate (US$ billion)	Scaling-up pathways: lessons learned and good practices
1. Improving tenure security over communal lands	0.40	• Organizing and formalizing communal groups • Demarcating boundaries and registering communal rights
2. Improving tenure security over individual lands	1.00	• Undertaking systematic titling with a spatial framework based on low-cost simple technology and without a boundary survey for low-value rural land • Undertaking systematic titling based on a detailed survey of boundaries for urban and high-value rural land
3. Increasing land access and tenure for the poor and vulnerable	0.50	• Redistributing rural land using a willing-seller willing-buyer approach • Regularizing rights of squatters on urban public land • Removing restrictions on land rental markets • Promoting gender equity with favorable laws and documentation of rights
4. Increasing efficiency and transparency in land administration services	1.30	• Decentralizing to empower local communities and traditional authorities, with clear provisions for social and financial sustainability • Computerizing and developing land information systems and national spatial data infrastructure • Modernizing surveying and mapping infrastructure, including geodetic referencing, base mapping, and cadastral systems
5. Developing capacity in land administration	0.40	• Undertaking institutional and policy reforms to guide capacity development • Undertaking training and knowledge transfer
6. Resolving land disputes and managing expropriations	0.20	• Resolving disputes by building competent institutions: strengthening judicial institutions and removing backlogs, creating specialized tribunals, training judges, and empowering alternative forums and approaches • Managing expropriations: updating laws, paying fair and full compensation, adhering to the principle of eminent domain, and improving the environment for governance

(continued next page)

5

Table 0.1 (continued)

Key element	Cost estimate (US$ billion)	Scaling-up pathways: lessons learned and good practices
7. Increasing scope and effectiveness of land use planning	0.40	• Anchoring land use planning in a national land policy • Preparing spatial planning frameworks at national, regional, and district levels to guide local planning in urban and rural areas • Preparing local land use plans in a participatory way using plans approved by democratically elected authorities
8. Improving public land management	0.10	• Inventorying, surveying, and registering all government lands • Ensuring that land not critical for public goods and services is allocated to the poor in a transparent process or to investors in a competitive process
9. Developing postconflict land administration	0.10	• Focusing on managing land-related conflicts early and developing land policies to address the underlying tensions after cessation of conflict • Encouraging that development partners deploy technical assistance early and rapidly to advise on resolution of policy issues • Reestablishing technical capacity to rebuild land administration • Using task forces and special commissions to fill the gap where governance institutions are weak or absent
10. Strengthening valuation functions and land tax policies	0.05	• Developing partnerships of government at all levels, driven by local governments • Providing local governments with access to better land administration services and information • Integrating essential elements of local revenue generation, including a sound tax policy, tax assessment system, and computerized tax collection system
Total	4.50[a]	

a. Amounts have been rounded up.

Improving Tenure Security over Communal Lands

The first element in the scaling-up program is "improving tenure security over communal lands," which are included among the 90 percent of unregistered rural lands in Sub-Saharan Africa. The scaling-up program aims to register all remaining communally owned land in most countries. While the land rights of community members were historically secure, this is no longer the case, as demand for communal land has surged, especially in the last 10 years, in response to increased private investment in natural resources. Land grabbing by private interests and expropriation without adequate compensation have been widely reported, with severe consequences, including the dispossession of local communities and rising investment risks (Deininger et al. 2011). Scaling up policies and investments in the registration of communal lands would help to protect the rights of local communities while reducing investment risks. The scaling up has two pathways.

Demarcating boundaries and registering communal rights   In Tanzania, the boundaries of village lands have been demarcated and community rights have been registered for about US$500 per community, confirming that community lands can be registered cost-effectively. This is consistent with international experience, especially that of Mexico. This book estimates that about US$400 million would be required to scale up the registration of communal lands in at least 30 countries. If communal rights were registered, the allocation and management of individual plots could be left to community institutions, with the option to register individual land rights as the need arises.

Organizing and formalizing communal groups   The scaling up of tenure security over communal lands also involves organizing and formalizing communal groups. These institution-building activities include (a) formulating by-laws to govern ways for communities to interact with outsiders and resolve conflicts and (b) enabling communities to enter into and honor agreements on land use with outsiders. Moreover, if the information from the demarcation of boundaries and the registration of communal rights could be maintained properly and made publicly accessible, this could considerably reduce the transaction costs for potential investors from outside the community and enhance the transparency of transactions. Combined with legal measures, this could reduce the neglect of existing rights that often accompanies land-related direct investment (Alden Wily 2010; Anseeuw et al. 2012). In addition, recognition of community rights and demarcation of relevant boundaries would aid international programs in countering global warming; for example, carbon offset programs of reforestation require documented land rights to identify and secure the rights of tree plantation owners.

Improving Tenure Security over Individual Lands

The second element in the scaling-up program is "improving tenure security over individual lands" by demarcating boundaries and registering land. This book estimates that registration of individually owned land can be scaled up from the current 10 percent to about 50 percent of rural lands, enough to cover prime agricultural lands in most Sub-Saharan African countries, at a cost of US$1 billion in at least 25 countries over 10 years. The scaling up has two pathways.

Systematic titling of low-value rural land using a spatial framework based on low-cost technology   While the proposed land registration is a huge task seen in historical perspective, it is manageable given the availability of lower-cost technologies (with their enhanced precision and accuracy) and the willingness of African governments to be flexible in selecting and applying surveying and mapping technologies. For example, using large-scale aerial orthophoto maps or rectified satellite imagery to describe and reference the boundaries of rural land in a systematic process can significantly reduce the cost and increase the speed of land registration. A nationwide program of land registration can now be completed within 5–10 years, while traditional approaches can take decades. Rwanda completed its national registration program (10.3 million parcels of land) in less than 5 years (in June 2012), using aerial orthophoto maps and rectified satellite imagery. Ethiopia registered 20 million parcels in 3 years (2003–05), without using a spatial framework such as a photomap. Madagascar, Namibia, and Tanzania piloted these low-cost technologies and are preparing to scale them up. These land titling programs, based on charting the boundaries

Landowners Participating in Systematic Land Titling in Bariadi District, Tanzania

Photo credit: ©Chris Mnyanga, land component coordinator, Private Sector Competitiveness Project, Tanzania.

of land parcels on photomaps, are much less expensive and faster than earlier land titling programs, which relied on detailed surveying of boundaries at a cost of at least US$50 per parcel (as opposed to US$10–US$20 per parcel or less for the new technologies).

Systematic titling based on a detailed survey of boundaries for urban and high-value rural land   In urban and periurban areas as well as rural areas of high commercial value, accurate measurement of boundaries is warranted by the high value of land. This requires conducting a detailed survey of boundaries in bulk, area by area, with systematic adjudication to increase transparency and reduce costs. While getting all landowners of the community to participate in systematic demarcation and adjudication is more difficult in urban than in rural areas, doing so is feasible, especially with good forward planning and dedicated education and awareness campaigns. Recent piloting of this approach in Ghana and Uganda was quite cost-effective at as low as US$32 per parcel in Ghana and US$23 per parcel in Uganda, compared with an average of US$25 per parcel in Thailand in the 1990s (World Bank 2003, 2004b; Burns 2007).

Scaling up the registration of land from 10 percent to 50 percent would have a considerable impact on the development of agriculture and the rest of the economy in Sub-Saharan Africa. It would improve land tenure security for individual landholders and, in turn, boost land-related investments, productivity, and gender equity if backed by a favorable regulatory framework, as was done in Ethiopia and Rwanda (Deininger, Ali, and Alemu 2011a; Ali, Deininger, and Goldstein 2011). In doing this, it would be following in the footsteps of China, which, in 1978, dismantled collective farms and used long-term leases to confer land rights on households, unleashing a period of prolonged growth in agricultural productivity that transformed rural China.

Land registration would also improve the fluidity of land markets, both sales and rental markets, which not only would transfer land to the most productive users as well as to youth, the poor, and the landless, but also would fuel the mobility of people and structural change. When more rewarding opportunities exist for off-farm activities, secure land rental markets can facilitate the migration of farmers from agriculture to other sectors, as they can lease out their land and get it back when they return. For example, in rural China, when land tenure security was strengthened during the 1980s and 1990s by eliminating the administrative reallocation of agricultural land and introducing land use certificates, millions of landowners rented their land to others and migrated to the booming coastal areas and cities where wages were more attractive (Deininger and Jin 2007). This enabled migrant workers to earn higher incomes off-farm and to rent their land for better uses.

Outside of the agriculture sector, scaled-up land registration combined with legal recognition of the rights of squatters on public land would have a considerable impact on the urban sector by enabling cities to function better. It would facilitate the development of efficient and equitable land markets, which would reduce business transaction costs and open up development opportunities for the 70 percent of the urban population now living in urban slums. All urban businesses and dwellers need secure access to land on which to operate or live productively. Among urban industries, the manufacturing sector would perhaps have the most to gain from land registration and the related increase in fluidity of the urban land market. According to Dinh et al. (2012), access to land is a constraint for most manufacturing firms in Sub-Saharan Africa. Small and large firms seeking to set up or expand a business face a lack of access to industrial land equipped with utilities and transport links to markets; they also lack land to use as collateral to secure loans.

Increasing Land Access and Tenure for the Poor and Vulnerable

The third element in the scaling-up program is "increasing land access and tenure for the poor and vulnerable," with an estimated cost of US$0.5 billion. The scaling up has four pathways.

Redistributing rural land   Landownership inequalities and landlessness are growing, and in Côte d'Ivoire, Kenya, Liberia, and Southern Africa they are high enough to undermine shared growth and social cohesion. Attempts have been made to address the problem not just in Africa, but the world over, through land redistribution and associated reforms with the aim of transferring land to the landless and land-poor segments of the population. While there is a general consensus on the need to redistribute land, there is often controversy about how to do so peacefully and legally, without invoking rampant corruption, political interference, rent seeking, or social conflict (Binswanger-Mkhize, Bourguignon, and van den Brink 2009). Mali has undertaken the most successful redistributive land reform in the region, though on a pilot basis.

To address the highly unequal distribution of overcrowded arable land, which coexists with underutilized large-scale farms, Malawi piloted a land reform program with funding from the World Bank (World Bank 2004a). The pilot project aimed to increase the income of about 15,000 rural poor families through a decentralized, community-based, and voluntary approach in four districts, modeled on Brazil's market-based approach to land reform (under implementation since the mid-1990s). The pilot had three key elements: (a) voluntary acquisition by communities of land sold by willing estate owners; (b) resettlement and on-farm development, including transportation of settlers, establishment of shelter, and purchase of basic inputs and advisory services; and (c) survey and registration of redistributed land. Land reform beneficiaries, organized in voluntary groups, were self-selected on the basis of predefined eligibility criteria. Each family received a grant of US$1,050, managed directly by beneficiaries, of which up to 30 percent was for land acquisition and the rest was for transportation, water, shelter, and farm development. Implementation was decentralized through District Assembly institutions and required capacity enhancement, especially for surveying and registration.

According to impact evaluation studies, the project achieved impressive results, including an increase of 40 percent in agricultural incomes for beneficiaries (compared to nonbeneficiaries) between 2005–06 and 2008–09; an economic rate of return of 20 percent; and positive impacts on the livelihoods of beneficiaries and surrounding communities, with improvements in land holdings, land tenure security, crop production, and productivity, and consequently on income and food security (Tchale 2012). These results leave no doubt that Malawi's redistributive land reform is a good model on which other countries can build in addressing landownership inequality and landlessness. This book estimates that about US$180 million would be required to build a strong foundation for land redistribution in six countries over 10 years.

South Africa has perhaps the most urgent need for land reform. Unlike in Malawi, land reform in South Africa has made slow progress in reducing ownership inequality and has had minimal impact on productivity and incomes. Started at the end of apartheid in 1994, South Africa's land reform program had transferred only 6.27 million hectares by March 2011, equivalent to 7.2 percent of the agricultural land under white ownership in 1994, leaving about 80 percent under white ownership (10 percent of the population); the current goal is to transfer 30 percent of white-owned agricultural land by 2025 (Lahiff and Li 2012).

Regularizing the rights of squatters on urban public land   According to the United Nations Population Fund (UNFPA 2011), 40 percent of Africa's population lives in cities, but 70 percent of those are in slum areas with poor living conditions. With rapid urbanization—half of the African population will be living in cities by 2050 (compared to about 38 percent in 2009)—land policies are critical for ensuring sustainable urban migration and economic growth in urban areas (African Union, African Development Bank, and UN Economic Commission for Africa 2009). The fast growth in urbanization and slum populations offers challenges for reducing poverty but also creates opportunities for boosting economic growth and improving services, taking advantage of the high population densities in urban and slum areas (World Bank 2008).

Since the 1960s, when governments embarked on failed programs to clear and replace squatter settlements with low-cost housing, numerous global initiatives have been undertaken to guide country-level interventions to improve living conditions in informal settlements. But country-level implementation has lagged behind and has focused primarily on upgrading infrastructure and services, neglecting regularization of land tenure or relegating it to pilots. More recently, there has been a movement toward adopting an integrated approach and scaling up land tenure regularization pilots. For example, Kenya has taken policy and constitutional measures to establish a firm legal framework for regularizing tenure security in informal settlements and has embarked on a large multidonor-funded program to regularize land tenure and upgrade the infrastructure of informal settlements in its 15 largest municipalities. Similarly, Tanzania has developed a legal framework and, with World Bank support, prepared a 10-year National Program for Regularization and Prevention of Unplanned Settlements, which takes an integrated approach to scaling up past efforts. Lesotho has developed the necessary legal framework and, with funding from the Millennium Challenge Corporation, is implementing a land tenure regularization program in Maseru (MCC 2011).

While the socioeconomic impacts of these programs have not yet been assessed, studies outside Africa have found significant positive impacts. For example, studies in some urban slums of Argentina, Indonesia, Peru, and the Philippines have found that regularization programs have positive and significant impacts on housing quality and on housing and land prices in areas covered by them compared to those not covered (Galiani and Schargrodsky 2005; Field 2005; Friedman, Jimenez, and Mayo 1988). A recent study in Tanzania found that regularizing land tenure using cost-effective systematic approaches would be affordable and produce benefits that exceed the costs (Ali et al. 2012).

In the context of Sub-Saharan Africa, the emerging approach to regularizing land tenure has six major elements: community education and participation on rights and responsibilities; adjudication and enumeration of rights of individuals and groups; agreement on and bulk survey of land boundaries; physical planning with wide community participation; adjustment of boundaries, walls, fences, and buildings to meet the agreed physical plan; and recognition of land rights in a local or central formal system or in a local informal or semiformal system. This emerging approach could form the basis for scaling up the regularization of land tenure across many countries in the region. There is potential to reduce costs through bulk planning and surveying as well as through low-cost approaches being piloted to capture information on land rights and through community-based approaches such as the Social Tenure Domain Model (Lemmen 2010) and "crowd sourcing" (Lemmen 2010; McLaren 2011). This book estimates that about US$300 million would be required to scale up the regularization of land tenure in urban slums in 30 countries over 10 years.

Removing restrictions on land rental markets   Land rental markets are a low-cost mechanism, requiring limited capital expenditure, for transferring land to the landless, the land poor, migrants, and young farmers; providing them with an opportunity to learn, practice, or strengthen their skills in farming; and helping them to move up the ladder toward landownership. Land rental markets have a long history in Sub-Saharan Africa, especially in West Africa, and have often provided a means to access land for commercial production such as cocoa farming in Ghana and to equalize farming operations (Amanor and Diderutuah 2001; Estudillo, Quisumbing, and Otsuka 2001). Case studies suggest that land rental markets have a positive impact on equity, benefiting the poor and women (Place 2002). Land rental markets can also enhance efficiency by transferring land from less to more productive users at low cost. In China, rental activity contributed to occupational diversification and increased productivity by about 60 percent (Deininger and Jin 2009).

Land rental markets are also important in driving labor mobility and enhancing the structural transformation of economies. For example, during the 1980s and 1990s, hundreds of millions of people migrated from agricultural to nonagricultural areas of China and Vietnam, associated with the transformation of their nonfarm economies. While this migration was driven by economic opportunities outside agriculture, it was facilitated by the emergence or strengthening of land rental and sales markets, underpinned by institutional strengthening of land rights. In rural China, more secure land tenure permitted existing landowners to rent their land to others and to migrate to the booming coastal areas and cities where wages were more attractive. The share of migrants in the labor force increased from 5 percent in 1988 to 17 percent in 2000, or a total of 124.6 million people; that figure is expected to reach 200 million by 2020 (Zhai, Hertel, and Wang 2003; Deininger and Jin 2007). The rapid migration led to a structural transformation of China's economy, with the share of agriculture in total employment declining from 70 percent in 1978 to 50 percent by 2000 (Johnson 2000).

At least two factors are critical for land rental markets to provide access for those who need land and can use it best, to enhance productivity and incomes, and to enhance structural transformation of Sub-Saharan African economies. The first factor is secure land tenure. Empirical studies show that improved land rights, through the introduction of long-term leases or the registration of land, have increased land rental activity in various countries, including China, the Dominican Republic, Ethiopia, Nicaragua, and Vietnam (Deininger and Feder 2009). Studies conducted in Ethiopia found that land certification programs in 1998–99 and 2003–05 resulted in higher rental market activities (Holden, Deininger, and Ghebru 2009; Deininger, Ali, and Alemu 2011b). The second factor is the avoidance or elimination of controls and restrictions on land rental markets. Experience in Uganda and Ethiopia suggests that even well-intended government controls and restrictions on land rental markets that are meant to avoid the exploitation of poor people can end up harming them. In Uganda, strict controls on rent and on the eviction of tenants drove landlords out of agricultural land rental markets during the 2000s (World Bank 2012c). In Ethiopia, restrictions on land rental markets in all regions except Amhara reduced the opportunities to put land to more productive uses (Deininger et al. 2003). For countries to boost land rental markets and their developmental benefits, it is important that governments strengthen land tenure security and eliminate restrictions on land rental as part of the scaling-up program.

Promoting gender equity with favorable laws and documentation of rights   A growing body of literature documents persistent gender gaps in African agriculture in particular and across the developing world in general (World Bank 2011g; Bezabih and Holden 2010; Peterman, Behrman, and Quisumbing 2010). Female farmers in many parts of the developing world face many challenges in accessing productive resources such as credit, fertilizer, and land. A comprehensive analysis of case studies from five South Asian countries showed that fewer women than men have command over the use of arable land, women have more limited land use rights, and many women have no control at all over production and management decisions (Agarwal 1994). The challenges facing women farmers in Africa are equally daunting. Women's rights to land and property are very limited and often depend on their marital status. It has been shown that improving access to productive resources such as fertilizer and land can improve women's agricultural yields by 10 to 30 percent. At the moment, African women farmers are less productive than their male counterparts; in Ethiopia, female farmers produce 26 percent less than male farmers, while in Ghana, they produce 17 percent less (FAO 2011; World Bank 2011g). More than 70 percent of farming activities in Africa are undertaken by women farmers, so improving the access of women to productive resources will invariably raise agricultural productivity and food security in many parts of Africa.

Women Working Land They Do Not Own in a Village in Rwanda

Photo credit: ©Jolly Dusabe, Rural Sector Support Program, Rwanda.

Legal recognition of women's land rights is the first step toward reversing the discrimination against women, and the constitutions and recent land-related laws of many countries recognize the equality of land rights (Deininger 2003). Implementation has been the primary challenge, given the discrimination ingrained in customary law. Ethiopia and Rwanda have risen to the challenge by implementing land registration programs that have successfully strengthened women's land rights. Impact evaluation studies of Ethiopia's registration program found that the program improved land tenure security for both men and women farmers and had a positive impact on productivity, although the magnitude of the gain was greater for men than for women, suggesting that women require better access to production inputs if they are to improve productivity (Deininger, Ali, and Alemu 2011a; Bezabih and Holden 2010). A study of the short-term impacts of Rwanda's registration program also found that the program improved land tenure security for women by improving access to land among legally married women and by prompting better gender-neutral recording of inheritance rights. The study also found that the program led to increased investment in and maintenance of soil conservation measures, particularly among female-headed households (Ali, Deininger, and Goldstein 2011).

Key interventions in Ethiopia and Rwanda included elevating women's secondary land rights to equal those of men, legally recognizing women's inheritance rights, and allowing the joint registration of spousal land rights. Supporting elements in such programs included education, awareness, and information campaigns highlighting women's land rights, adequate representation of women on program implementation teams, and open and accessible appeal systems for addressing the concerns of aggrieved parties. The design, implementation, and results of the Ethiopian and Rwandan land registration programs imply that, when properly scaled up, these programs can reduce existing gender gaps, thereby addressing cultural biases and historical shortcomings of land policies in many parts of Sub-Saharan Africa. These are excellent examples that other countries can emulate in scaling up their programs.

Increasing Efficiency and Transparency in Land Administration Services

The fourth element for scaling up is "increasing efficiency and transparency in land administration services." This element involves the most countries (about 40) and will cost the most (about 30 percent of the total cost): about US$1.3 billion. The huge scale-up is warranted by the degree of effort required to overhaul land administration systems and infrastructure to boost efficiency and transparency from their currently low levels. For example, it takes twice as long and costs twice as much (65 days and 9.4 percent of property value, respectively) to transfer land in Sub-Saharan Africa as it does in OECD countries (31 days and 4.4 percent). Regarding the problem of transparency, a study in 61 countries by property from 227 days in 2007 to 48 days in 2011 by combining computerization with rehabilitation of manual land registers and other reforms, especially in property valuation (World Bank 2012b).

While computerization and development of LISs generate considerable benefits, the vast majority of developing countries still use paper-based systems and obsolete routines to register land: more than 80 percent of Sub-Saharan African and South Asian countries still have paper-based systems that are in deteriorated conditions (World Bank 2012b). Similarly, national spatial data infrastructure (NSDI), which is necessary to harmonize and share land information, is lacking in many developing countries, including those in Sub-Saharan Africa. Such infrastructure takes time to develop. For example, a recent review of Kenya's initiative to establish NSDI indicates that, after 10 years and considerable expense, the only notable achievement was the development of NSDI standards; neither an NSDI policy nor legislation had been officially adopted, and problems with sharing spatial data persisted (Oloo 2011). The Kenya experience highlights that, among other things, formulating and implementing an NSDI program can be a long-term venture. It also suggests that Kenya could have benefited from lessons and guiding principles derived from global experience, including (a) starting with a policy and legislation to guide the development of NSDI; (b) focusing initially on specific areas of application, even while starting to build longer-term generic architecture; (c) building on existing structures and institutional arrangements; and (d) engaging all stakeholders (GIC/ESRI Canada 2011). The scaling-up program supported by this book will enable the majority of Sub-Saharan African countries to replace their paper-based systems with more efficient and transparent computerized systems and to develop NSDI within 10 years.

Modernizing surveying and mapping infrastructure   The vast majority of countries in Sub-Saharan Africa have not upgraded their infrastructure for land administration since independence. Surveying and mapping infrastructure are typically outdated, including geodetic reference frameworks, cartographic machinery for producing maps, and infrastructure for sharing maps and other spatial data. The outdated infrastructure has lost not only its relevance to today's needs but also its productivity and efficiency. It is partly responsible for the high cost of cadastral surveying, which, when done on demand, is in excess of US$200 per parcel in countries such as Ghana, Tanzania, and Uganda. This is much higher than the US$50 or less per parcel in Central and Eastern Europe, where investment in technology such as global navigational satellite system (GNSS) reference frameworks has reduced the capital investment and operating costs required for cadastral surveying.

Many countries are aware of the importance of having up-to-date infrastructure for land administration and have undertaken initiatives to modernize their in remote provinces were still referring to previous land codes, completely unaware of the new law.

In response to such problems, Mozambique is notable for having put in place the most sustained effort to date to enhance the ability of the judiciary to implement land-related laws. For most of the last decade, the Center for Judicial Training in Maputo has hosted an intensive course for sitting and in-training judges on three innovative laws adopted in the 1990s—the Land Law, the Forestry Law, and the Law on Environment. The need for such training arose from clear recognition that the adjudication of cases arising under these laws required a radical reorientation in judicial thinking, away from applying state law alone to determining and recognizing the legitimacy of community-based rule systems in certain situations. The effectiveness of Mozambique's training strategy is difficult to measure, but even in the absence of empirical validation, such efforts are clearly necessary, if not sufficient.

The recent paradigm shift in thinking about land relations in Africa— embodied by the passage of new land laws—has among its guiding principles that land disputes are often better managed and adjudicated in accordance with customary norms and processes than by state institutions alone. In other words, legal pluralism is to be embraced rather than shunned. Related to this is recognition that effective resolution of land disputes requires mechanisms that are closer and more accessible to the people who need them and better attuned to local realities. Kenya's national land policy calls "as far as possible" for ADR mechanisms such as negotiation, mediation, and arbitration to facilitate fair and accessible justice on land matters (United Republic of Kenya 2009). The new Kenyan constitution explicitly encourages communities "to settle land disputes through recognized local community initiatives consistent with this Constitution" (United Republic of Kenya 2010). To a large extent, such provisions simply express what is already happening on the ground—the vast majority of land disputes are already settled (or continue to fester unresolved) at local levels, outside of formal legal processes.

As important and attractive as this shift is, there are considerable challenges in supporting its implementation in a way that remains true to the twin objectives of transparent and equitable dispute resolution, on the one hand, and application of local norms and decision-making processes, on the other. A growing emphasis on the role of local and community-based institutions in land administration comes at a time when, in many parts of Africa, such institutions are themselves evolving rapidly—and in some cases weakening—in the face of social and economic pressures.

Ghana again provides a good example. Its constitution and national land policy recognize customary ownership of land and the operation of customary law; they also recognize the critical importance of traditional authorities in the decentralized administration of land and the potential for establishing customary land secretariats (CLSs) to provide a locally tailored mechanism for managing land and resolving disputes. Under a multidonor-funded project, support was provided for the establishment of CLSs in 37 traditional authorities in Ghana (World Bank 2011b). CLSs are responsible for several important elements, including dispute resolution. To date, the CLSs experience has been mixed. While there have been several notable successes, in other cases CLSs have not taken root due to lack of interest or weak capacity. The tensions inherent in CLSs between the importance of local decision making and dispute resolution, on the one hand, and the dangers of elite capture, on the other, have become particularly exposed in recent years in response to the growing commercialization of land. While by custom and constitutional stipulation the chief is a trustee of land for his community, chiefs have often assumed the role of landowner, striking deals with outsiders without consulting with or obtaining approval from community members.

The foregoing is not intended to deflect attention from the importance of empowering locally based forums for managing and resolving land disputes. It does, however, strike a cautionary note—namely, that supporting effective and legitimate local dispute resolution should not be automatically equated with supporting idealized customary institutions. More generally, the appropriateness of ADR is clearly not universal.

Managing expropriations   All governments worldwide, including those in Sub-Saharan Africa, possess the power to acquire land involuntarily for a public purpose or use, usually subject to the payment of fair compensation. This power is an essential development tool—governments cannot always depend on markets to ensure the availability of land to meet critical development priorities. At the same time, it is almost always a flash point for controversy. Even when generous compensation is paid, involuntary taking of land can disrupt livelihoods and communities. When the process is handled badly, it can foster corruption, distort land markets, undermine tenure security, and trigger social unrest.

The legal frameworks governing compulsory acquisition in Sub-Saharan Africa are derived from a variety of common and civil law sources and hence vary significantly from country to country. Nevertheless, certain challenges have relevance for many parts of the subcontinent. One overarching observation is that legal approaches developed in Europe or North America—where land rights are generally standardized and well defined, land markets function well, and land records are reliable—are not suitable in contexts where such attributes are less common (Keith et al. 2008).

A review of experience with compulsory acquisition in this book suggests that tackling problems in land acquisition and compensation requires multiple actions:

20 countries over 10 years. Land use planning is important to ensure that land is used in the best interests of society. While the state has an important role in protecting the land rights of its citizens, it also has a responsibility to protect the social or public interest when individuals' land use decisions are detrimental to the public interest. State intervention is justified when the actions of individual land users negatively affect landscapes, biodiversity, historic sites, or cultural values (Deininger 2003). The common mode of intervention is land use planning and restrictions (regulations), which are important not only to ensure effective management of land use but also to provide infrastructure and public services, improve the urban and rural environment, prevent pollution, and pursue sustainable development (Williamson et al. 2010). In developing countries and Sub-Saharan Africa in particular, where customary land tenure is predominant, land use planning has also become important to (a) identify and delineate surplus land for investors and (b) delineate and facilitate improved group management of communally owned, pastoral, or protected lands. Socially desirable government interventions for land use planning and restrictions require adequate "implementation capacity, transparent and fair allocation of costs and benefits, and predictable rules designed to minimize compliance costs" (Deininger 2003). The proposed scaling up of land use planning has three pathways.

Anchoring land use planning in a national land policy An important challenge to policy makers is to balance landowners' rights with the necessity and capacity of government to regulate land use in the best interests of society, a

Villagers Participating in the Preparation of Village Land Use Plans in Bariadi District, Tanzania

Photo credit: ©Chris Mnyanga, land component coordinator, Private Sector Competitiveness Project, Tanzania.

balance that can only be formalized in a national land policy developed with broad and deep consultations and implemented in a highly participatory manner (Williamson et al. 2010). Ghana's and Tanzania's land use planning processes strike a reasonable balance between protecting private property rights and the public interest while also promoting sustainable development by underpinning the planning process with national land policies adopted after broad consultations (World Bank 2003, 2005b).

Preparing spatial planning frameworks to guide local planning   Spatial planning frameworks are prepared at national, regional, and district levels to guide lower-level planning. They should indicate present and future major land uses, conservation areas and transportation networks, boundaries of special planning concern, and directions for further growth. While spatial planning frameworks are not legal documents, they must still be approved by the appropriate authorities.

Making local land use plans participatory and approved by democratically elected authorities   Local plans identify detailed land uses at the parcel level, with strong community participation. They are legal documents and must be approved by local authorities and form the basis for issuing planning and building permits in urban areas. Ghana's and Tanzania's planning models are similar, and both include spatial planning frameworks and local land use plans. Approval of land use plans by democratically elected authorities (in addition to technical authorities) and community participation in local land use plans help to protect landowners' rights, on the one hand, and to regulate land use in the best interests of society, on the other. Ghana's and Tanzania's experiences should serve other countries well as they scale up their efforts. Obviously, each country will develop planning guidelines that are suitable for its own unique conditions. Generic planning guidelines such as those developed by United Nations Habitat's Global Land Tool Network (UN-Habitat, GLTN 2010) can be of help to the exercise.

Improving Public Land Management

The eighth element to scale up is "improving public land management," at an estimated cost of US$0.10 billion, enough to cover at least 10 countries over 10 years. State landownership is widespread in Sub-Saharan Africa. Many countries inherited legal provisions at independence that promoted the concept of public land, including unused customary land, which governments readily used or simply claimed. Countries with colonial white settlements, especially in Kenya and Southern Africa, nationalized settlers' farmlands and corporate farms after independence. During the 1970s, others, including Benin, Burkina Faso, Nigeria, and Uganda, either nationalized private and customary lands or established a state monopoly over land allocation, using this as a carte blanche to expand state landownership; this often created conditions for high levels

Investing in Land Conservation Encouraged by Land Tenure Security in Tanzania

Photo credit: ©Emma Isinika-Modamba, World Bank Country Office, Tanzania.

Poverty Reduction

In addition to economic growth, scaling up comprehensive land reforms and investments will contribute to poverty reduction more directly by redistributing underused land to those who are land poor, removing restrictions on rental markets for agricultural land, increasing women's access to land, and regularizing land tenure for urban squatters on public land. This book has documented evidence that interventions in these areas have had positive impacts on shared growth and poverty reduction, including redistributive land reform in Malawi; removal of restrictions in land rental markets in China, Ethiopia, Vietnam, and West Africa; regularization of land tenure in East Asia and Latin America; and increased gender equality in landownership in Ethiopia and Rwanda.

Conflict Management, Sustainable Development, and Decentralized Governance

In addition, scaling up reforms and investments in land administration will support development in other ways. In postconflict countries, scaled-up early interventions in developing land administration will prevent and improve management of recurring conflicts associated with land and generate peace dividends, as results documented in this book suggest, especially for Liberia and Rwanda. Scaling up land use planning, long neglected in Sub-Saharan African countries, will promote sustainable urbanization, improve management of common property resources, and facilitate sustainable exploitation of natural resources, including agricultural land, forests, water, and minerals. Additional benefits of scaling up would come from modernization of land administration systems, especially for property valuation and land information, which, combined with improved land tax policies, will generate increased land-related revenue, necessary to enhance local governance and sustain land administration.

Note

1. They include Benin, Botswana, Burkina Faso, Ghana, Kenya, Madagascar, Malawi, Mali, Mauritius, Namibia, Nigeria, Rwanda, Senegal, Tanzania, Uganda, and Zambia.

References

African Union, African Development Bank, and UN (United Nations) Economic Commission for Africa. 2009. *Framework and Guidelines on Land Policy in Africa: Land Policy in Africa; A Framework to Strengthen Land Rights, Enhance Productivity, and Secure Livelihoods.* Addis Ababa: African Union, African Development Bank, and UN Economic Commission for Africa.

African Union, UN Economic Commission for Africa, and African Development Bank. n.d. "Draft Elements of a Five-Year LPI Strategic Plan and Roadmap (2012–2016)." African Union, African Development Bank, and UN Economic Commission for Africa, Addis Ababa.

Agarwal, B. 1994. *A Field of One's Own: Gender and Land Rights in South Asia.* South Asian Studies. New York: Cambridge University Press.

Ahene, R. 2012. "A Review of Government Land Inventories in Ghana and Uganda." Working Paper for the "Land Administration and Reform in SSA" study, World Bank, Washington, DC.

Alden Wily, L. 2010. "Whose Land Are You Giving Away, Mr. President?" Paper presented at the Annual Bank Conference on Land Policy and Administration, Washington, DC, April 26–27.

Ali, D. A., K. Deininger, S. Dercon, M. Hunter, J. Sanderfur, and A. Zeitlin. 2012. "Are Poor Slum-Dwellers Willing to Pay for Formal Land Title? Evidence from Dar es Salaam." Working Paper, World Bank, Washington, DC.

Ali, D., K. Deininger, and M. Goldstein. 2011. "Environmental and Gender Impacts of Land Tenure Regularization in Africa: Pilot Evidence from Rwanda." Policy Research Working Paper 5765, World Bank, Washington, DC.

Amanor, K. S., and M. K. Diderutuah. 2001. "Share Contracts in the Oil Palm and Citrus Belt of Ghana." International Institute for Environment and Development, London.

Anseeuw, W., L. Alden Wily, L. Cotula, and M. Taylor. 2012. "Land Rights and the Rush for Land: Findings of the Global Commercial Pressures on Land Research Project." International Land Coalition, Rome.

Arial, A., C. Fagan, and W. Zimmermann. 2011. "Corruption in the Land Sector." IT Working Paper 04/2011, FAO and Transparency International, Berlin.

Bezabih, M., and S. Holden. 2010. "The Role of Land Certification in Reducing Gender Gaps in Productivity in Rural Ethiopia: Environment for Development." EFD Discussion Paper, RFF Press, Washington, DC, November.

Binswanger-Mkhize, H. P., C. Bourguignon, and R. van den Brink, eds. 2009. *Agricultural Land Redistribution: Toward Greater Consensus*. Washington, DC: World Bank.

Bird, R. M., and E. Slack. 2004. *International Handbook on Land and Property Taxation*. Cheltenham, U.K.: Edward Edgar Publishing.

Brits, A. M., C. Grant, and T. Burns. 2002. "Comparative Study of Land Administration Systems with Special Reference to Thailand, Indonesia, and Karnataka (India)." Paper presented at the World Bank Regional Land Workshop, Phnom Penh, June 4–6.

Bruce, J. 2012. "Land Administration Challenges in Post-Conflict States in Sub-Saharan Africa: Lessons from Rwanda and Liberia." Working Paper for the "Land Administration and Reforms in SSA" study, World Bank, Washington, DC.

Bruce, J. W., and A. Knox. 2009. "Structures and Stratagems: Decentralization of Authority over Land in Africa." *World Development* (special issue on the limits of state-led land reform) 37 (8): 1360–69.

Brueckner, J. K. 2000. "Fiscal Decentralization in Developing Countries: The Effects of Local Corruption and Tax Evasion." *Annals of Economics and Finance* 1 (1): 1–18.

Burns, T. 2007. "Land Administration Reform: Indicators of Success and Future Challenges." Agriculture and Rural Development Discussion Paper 37, World Bank, Washington, DC.

Cotula, L., S. Vermeulen, R. Leonard, and J. Keeley. 2009. "Land Grab or Development Opportunity? Agricultural Investment and International Land Deals in Africa." International Institute for Environment and Development, London; FAO, Rome; International Fund for Agricultural Development, Rome.

Deininger, K. 2003. *Land Policies for Growth and Poverty Reduction*. World Bank Policy Research Report. Washington, DC: World Bank; New York: Oxford University Press.

———. 2008. "A Strategy for Improving Land Administration in India." Land Policy and Administration Note 33, Agriculture and Rural Development, World Bank, February.

Deininger, K., D. A. Ali, and T. Alemu. 2011a. "Impacts of Land Certification on Tenure Security, Investment, and Land Market Participation: Evidence from Ethiopia." *Land Economics* 87 (2): 312–34.

———. 2011b. "Productivity Effects of Land Rental Markets in Ethiopia: Evidence from a Matched Tenant-Landlord Sample." Policy Research Working Paper 5727, World Bank, Washington, DC.

Deininger, K., D. Byerlee, J. Lindsay, A. Norton, H. Selod, and M. Stickler. 2011. *Rising Global Interest in Farmland: Can It Yield Sustainable and Equitable Benefits?* Washington, DC: World Bank.

Deininger, K., and G. Feder. 2009. "Land Registration, Governance, and Development: Evidence and Implications for Policy." *World Bank Research Observer* 24 (2): 233–66.

Deininger, K., and S. Jin. 2007. "Land Rental Markets in the Process of Rural Structural Transformation: Productivity and Equity Impacts in China." Policy Research Working Paper 4454, World Bank, Washington, DC.

report submitted to the Agrarian Sector Technical Review Group and World Bank, Washington, DC.

Sikor, T., and D. Muller. 2009. "The Limits of State-Led Land Reform: An Introduction." *World Development* (special issue on the limits of state-led land reform) 37 (8): 1307–16.

Tanner, C. 2002. "Law Making in an African Context: The 1997 Mozambican Land Law." Legal Papers Online 26, Food and Agriculture Organization of the United Nations. http://www.fao.org/Legal/Prs-OL/lpo26.pdf.

Tchale, H. 2012. "Pilot Redistributive Land Reform in Malawi: Innovations and Emerging Good Practices." Working Paper for the "Land Administration and Reform in SSA" study, World Bank, Washington, DC.

Torhonen, M. P., and D. Palmer. 2004. "Land Administration in Post-Conflict Cambodia." Paper presented at the symposium "Post-Conflict Land Administration Areas," Geneva, April 29–30.

UNFPA (United Nations Population Fund). 2011. *The State of World Population 2011: People and Possibilities in a World of 7 Billion.* New York: UNFPA.

UN (United Nations)-Habitat, GLTN (Global Land Tool Network). 2010. *Citywide Strategic Planning: A Guideline.* Nairobi: United Nations Print Shop. http://www.gltn.net/en/home/land-use-planning/citywide-strategic-planning-guidelines/details.html.

———. 2011. "Land and Property Tax: A Policy Guide." UN-Habitat, GLTN, Nairobi, October 8. http://www.gltn.net/en/home/land-tax-and-valuation/land-and-property-tax-a-policy-guide/download.html.

United Republic of Kenya. 2009. "Sessional Paper No. 3 of 2009 on National Land Policy, August 2009." Government Printer for the Ministry of Lands, Nairobi.

———. 2010. "The Constitution of Kenya 2010." National Council for Law Reporting, Nairobi.

Williamson, I., S. Enemark, J. Wallace, and A. Rajabffard. 2010. *Land Administration for Sustainable Development.* Redlands, CA: ESRI Press Academic.

World Bank. 2003. "Ghana Land Administration Project." Project Appraisal Document, World Bank, Washington, DC.

———. 2004a. "Malawi Community-Based Rural Land Development Project." Project Appraisal Document, World Bank, Washington, DC.

———. 2004b. "Uganda Second Private Sector Competitiveness Project." Project Appraisal Document, World Bank, Washington, DC.

———. 2005a. "Tanzania Private Sector Competitiveness Project." Project Appraisal Document, World Bank, Washington, DC.

———. 2005b. "Uganda Private Sector Competitiveness Project II, Land Component Project Implementation Manual." World Bank, Washington, DC.

———. 2007. *World Development Report 2008: Agriculture for Development.* Washington, DC: World Bank.

———. 2008. *World Development Report 2009: Reshaping Economic Geography.* Washington, DC: World Bank.

least between members of the community (Bruce and Mighot-Adholla 1994). Moreover, title deeds do not necessarily turn an insecure situation into a secure one; their efficacy depends on the context, and property rights can be secured in other ways, such as by providing freehold, leasehold, and certificates of varying rights, thereby forming a continuum of upgradable rights for individuals as well as communities (van den Brink et al. 2006). Some countries have applied this flexible approach to documenting land rights; the experiences and their associated impacts are reviewed and presented in later chapters of this book. Consensus has also been reached on the need to address the unequal distribution of land in a peaceful way, using a suite of instruments that includes market- and community-assisted approaches, not just compulsory acquisition (Binswanger-Mkhize, Bourguignon, and van den Brink 2009). Several initiatives being implemented in Africa under this model are also reviewed in this book.

Many African countries have either legislation in place or initiatives under way to address gender equality and communal land rights. However, legislating and enforcing these secondary rights can be challenging—for example, the right of herders to use land temporarily for grazing after harvest or the right of villagers (especially women and the poor) to collect firewood, forest food products, medicinal plants, and building materials on land previously owned communally. When entities from different communities claim conflicting land use rights, as happens with mobile pastoralists and sedentary farmers, simply documenting communal land rights community by community, as is commonly done in Sub-Saharan Africa, will not solve the problem. Rather, the solution requires a combination of (a) clearly documenting communal rights (as private property rights) and (b) addressing the rights of individual stakeholders using stronger community-level negotiations and dispute resolution mechanisms (Alden Wily 2008).

In addition to the challenges of documenting secondary and communal land rights, there are new and urgent demands to scale up documentation of land rights. The first demand is due to the so-called land grab, dubbed by some as the "second scramble for Africa" (Cotula et al. 2009). The land grab began as a major rise in investor interest in agricultural land following the 2008 food and commodity price boom: more than 1 million hectares of land were acquired in 2004–09 in each of at least four African countries—Ethiopia, Liberia, Mozambique, and Sudan (Deininger et al. 2011). While this surge in investment in large-scale agriculture has the potential to increase productivity and economic growth, with associated benefits for local communities, serious concerns have been raised about the neglect of local land rights and the failure to generate satisfactory benefits for local communities (Deininger et al. 2011; Cotula et al. 2009). For governments to reduce the real risk of dispossessing local communities while ensuring the certainty of deals negotiated by investors, it is both critical and urgent that land rights in Africa be documented and that land institutions and land delivery systems be strengthened.

The second recent demand for documenting land rights is due to the requirements of carbon offset reforestation programs being promoted to counter global warming. For these programs to work, the rights of tree plantation owners need to be identified and secured.

While the magnitude and urgency of documenting land rights are daunting, the process should be manageable given the availability of new lower-cost technologies (with their enhanced precision and accuracy) and the willingness of African governments to be more flexible in selecting and applying surveying and mapping technologies. For example, the use of large-scale aerial orthophotos or rectified satellite imagery to describe and reference the boundaries of rural land in a systematic registration process can significantly reduce the cost and increase the speed of land registration; a nationwide program of land registration can now be completed within 5 to 10 years, while traditional approaches can take decades.

Global Experiences and the Piloting of Innovations in Sub-Saharan Africa

While land issues and their solutions tend to be local in nature, it helps to understand and learn from global experiences, both good and bad. This book highlights some global approaches to land registration being piloted in Sub-Saharan African countries, including (a) systematic adjudication and registration using fast and cost-effective cadastral survey techniques,[1] (b) group or community titling, and (c) market-assisted redistribution of land to increase the agricultural incomes of the poor.

Countries that have successfully undertaken nationwide programs of land registration in the shortest time possible and at low cost have, in general, done so using simple cadastral surveys, producing standard graphical cadastral index maps to demarcate, adjudicate, and register land systematically (area by area). For example, Thailand undertook a nationwide program to register its land over a 20-year period in four 5-year phases starting in 1984. As of the end of 2011, Thailand had registered about 30 million full titles and an additional 30 million lower-grade titles. The spatial framework for titling was mainly orthophoto maps produced from aerial photography. In 2009, after careful piloting, Rwanda embarked on a nationwide program to register its lands using photomaps produced from aerial photography and high-resolution satellite imagery. The program was completed in June 2012, after demarcating all of its estimated 10.3 million parcels (in less than five years), at a cost per parcel of about US$10.

Ethiopia, Madagascar, Namibia, and Tanzania are piloting a similar methodology and plan to scale up in the near future.

There is a long history worldwide of land reforms to address the extremely unequal and often inefficient distribution of landownership. Central and South America initiated land reforms after World War I, and Asian economies (China; Japan; the Republic of Korea; the Philippines; and Taiwan, China) undertook their reforms during and immediately after World War II. Land reforms in the Arab Republic of Egypt, Kenya, South Africa, and Zimbabwe began in the 1950s and are still continuing (Deininger 2003). Land reform can be justified on efficiency and equity grounds as a strategy to provide access to productive assets, but its success relies on also providing beneficiaries with access to working capital and assets other than land that enable them to use land productively.

In that vein, the redistributive land reform most relevant for countries in Sub-Saharan Africa is the community-based land reform implemented by Brazil starting in the mid-1990s. Brazil's program aimed to avoid compulsory acquisition and instead relied on voluntary negotiation of prices between willing sellers and willing buyers (the WSWB approach). The government of Brazil gave poor farmers loans to acquire and develop land and provided grants for community infrastructure under a highly decentralized program. The 1990s program was preceded by the introduction of a land tax and a reduction of incentives for large holdings meant to induce large landholders to put their excess land on the market. Poor farmers were organized into groups that negotiated and obtained land as a group. In less than 10 years, this program benefited more than half a million households, more than the number helped over the previous 30 years by the compulsory acquisition program. While the success was partly attributed to increased funding by the government, the community-based land reform program transferred land faster than the previous program and at half the cost per household (Deininger 2003). Beneficiaries' incomes increased substantially as well. Due to its demonstrated success, similar community-based programs have been piloted in Sub-Saharan Africa, notably in Malawi, where it has been successful, and in South Africa, with less success.

Other innovations being piloted include rural land use plans (*plans foncier ruraux*) in Benin, Burkina Faso, and Côte d'Ivoire; demarcation and registration of communal lands in Ghana, Mozambique, and Tanzania; regularization of land tenure in urban informal settlements in Kenya, Lesotho, and Tanzania; identification, demarcation, and registration of government lands in Ghana and Uganda; construction of national geodetic networks based on continuously operating reference stations in Ghana and using global navigational satellite systems–based passive stations in Tanzania; and development of integrated land information systems using open-source software in Ghana and proprietary software in Uganda. The progress of these innovative pilots and their readiness for scaling up are discussed later in this book.

Readiness to Scale Up to Meet Demand

Countries in Sub-Saharan Africa seem poised to scale up their engagement in several areas of land administration and reform. Doing so would increase access to land for the poor by facilitating rental markets, redistributing underused agricultural land, and regularizing land tenure in urban slums. It also would increase efficiency in the delivery of land services and information by developing enhanced infrastructure, systems, and capacity for land administration.

The first indication of readiness to scale up is that pilot projects implemented over many years have positioned countries well to learn from their own experiences. The second indication of readiness is that many countries have put in place core land policies and laws to address long-standing issues such as recognizing customary tenure and ensuring women's land rights (Alden Wily 2012).

The third indication of readiness to scale up is that many countries have undertaken reforms to transform their land delivery institutions and systems to make them transparent and efficient. Based on the World Bank's annual Doing Business reports, countries in Sub-Saharan Africa have been at the forefront of implementing reforms to reduce the time, cost, and procedures for transferring property: during 2005–11, Sub-Saharan Africa recorded the highest number of reforms (49) making it easier to register property, followed by Europe and Central Asia, with 34 reforms. South Asia was last, with only 9 reforms (see table 1.1).

Table 1.1 Number of Doing Business Reforms Making It Easier to Register Property, 2005–11

Region	Number of economies	Total number of reforms
Sub-Saharan Africa	46	49
Eastern Europe and Central Asia	24	34
OECD (high income)	31	30
Latin America and the Caribbean	32	24
Middle East and North Africa	18	12
East Asia and Pacific	24	11
South Asia	8	9

Source: World Bank 2011.
Note: An economy can only be considered to have one Doing Business reform per topic and year. The sample for Doing Business in 2006 (World Bank 2005) includes 174 economies. The sample for Doing Business 2012 (World Bank 2011) added The Bahamas, Bahrain, Brunei Darussalam, Cyprus, Kosovo, Liberia, Luxembourg, Montenegro, and Qatar, for a total of 183 economies. OECD = Organisation for Economic Co-operation and Development.

Notwithstanding past reforms, there is still a long way to go. For example, it takes 65 days to complete a property transfer in Sub-Saharan Africa compared to 31 days in Organisation for Economic Co-operation and Development (OECD) countries, and the cost of the transfer (excluding informal payments) is 9.4 percent of the property value—more than twice as high as in OECD countries, where it is 4.4 percent (World Bank 2011).

The fourth indication of readiness to scale up is that, while capacity is still generally weak, many countries have a critical mass of trained people, both in the public and in the private sectors, to implement scaled-up programs in the land sector. In addition, Sub-Saharan Africa can call on its diaspora to bring home experiences acquired internationally.

The fifth indication of readiness to scale up is that African governments have made a commitment to implement more land policy reforms, primarily second-generation reforms. In their July 2009 summit in Sirte, Libya, the African Heads of State and Government adopted a declaration to develop and implement comprehensive land policies, guided by the African Union's *Framework and Guidelines on Land Policy in Africa,* which African institutions worked on collaboratively for three years (African Union, African Development Bank, and UN Economic Commission for Africa 2009). African countries share the global United Nations commitment to improving land policies and governance of tenure, including playing a leading role in the intergovernmental negotiations of the *Voluntary Guidelines on the Responsible Governance of Tenure of Land, Fisheries, and Forests in the Context of National Food Security* (FAO 2012; see box 1.1). With this collective commitment to do more, countries deserve support for scaling up, including not only financial resources but also information needed to evaluate and draw lessons from past initiatives, to appraise and select appropriate technologies, and to track performance and measure impacts.

BOX 1.1

The Voluntary Guidelines on Governance of Tenure

The *Voluntary Guidelines on the Responsible Governance of Tenure of Land, Fisheries, and Forests in the Context of National Food Security* is the first comprehensive instrument on tenure and its administration to be developed by governments through negotiations conducted in the United Nations system. The guidelines are based on an inclusive consultation process started by the Food and Agriculture Organization (FAO) in 2009 and finalized through intergovernmental negotiations led by the Committee on World Food Security. Their development included the participation of civil society

(continued next page)

Box 1.1 (continued)

organizations, private sector representatives, international organizations, and academics. The committee officially endorsed the guidelines at its 38th (special) session on May 11, 2012.

Being voluntary, the guidelines are not legally binding and do not replace existing national or international laws and commitments, nor do they limit or undermine any legal obligations that states may have under international law. While the voluntary nature of international "soft law" instruments such as the guidelines are sometimes considered to be a weakness, these instruments often have advantages over binding international instruments. It is usually easier for countries to reach agreements on voluntary instruments than on binding ones, which allows voluntary instruments to be more comprehensive. As a result, voluntary instruments such as the guidelines are usually better suited for technical matters. The FAO's experience is that voluntary instruments have had a positive impact on guiding national policies and laws in many countries.

The guidelines aim to promote food security and sustainable development by improving secure access to land, fisheries, and forests and by protecting the tenure rights of millions of people, who are often very poor. The guidelines provide a global consensus, having been prepared through negotiations involving governments of countries from all regions of the world with diverse political, economic, social, cultural, and religious views and with the final text reflecting ideas put forward by civil society and private sector organizations.

African countries played an active role in the negotiations, working together as a regional block. Perceiving the guidelines as an opportunity to support its work, the secretariat of the Land Policy Initiative provided technical assistance to the negotiators from African countries based on the principles set out in the *Framework and Guidelines on Land Policy in Africa*.

The guidelines set out internationally accepted principles and standards for responsible practices of tenure. They address a wide range of issues:

• Recognizing and protecting legitimate tenure rights, even under informal systems

• Setting out best practices for registering and transferring tenure rights

• Making sure that land administration systems are accessible and affordable

• Managing expropriations and restitution of land to people who were forcibly evicted in the past

• Ensuring the tenure rights of indigenous communities

• Ensuring that investments in agricultural lands occur responsibly and transparently

• Providing mechanisms for resolving disputes over tenure rights

• Dealing with the expansion of cities into rural areas.

Source: FAO 2012.

Objectives and Structure of the Book

This book synthesizes evaluations of recent experiences in implementing land policies and the technologies used, as well as the impacts of reforming land tenure and access. Its primary objective is to equip African decision makers and their development partners with the tools, best practices, and lessons learned that they need to respond to the increased demand for interventions to improve land governance and equity in ownership. Another objective is to generate and share knowledge with a broader international audience to foster broad-based support for reforms in land distribution and administration.

Chapter 2 reviews Sub-Saharan African experiences with documenting land rights and the subsequent impacts. Chapter 3 examines land reform in the context of improving land access for the poor. Chapter 4 evaluates experiences in addressing governance issues and managing conflict through reforms in land administration. Chapters 5 and 6 review experiences in modernizing the infrastructure (hardware) and systems (software) for land administration, respectively. Chapter 7 concludes by reviewing implications of the book's findings for scaling up investments by African governments to strengthen land governance and improve equity in landownership.

Note

1. Cadastral surveying refers to the field and office procedures used to survey and chart the boundaries of land parcels and other cadastral information as well as the procedures used to maintain this spatial information.

References

African Union, African Development Bank, and UN (United Nations) Economic Commission for Africa. 2009. *Framework and Guidelines on Land Policy in Africa: Land Policy in Africa; A Framework to Strengthen Land Rights, Enhance Productivity, and Secure Livelihoods.* African Union, African Development Bank, and UN Economic Commission for Africa, Addis Ababa.

Alden Wily, L. 2008. "Custom and Commonage in Africa Rethinking the Orthodoxies." *Land Use Policy Journal* 25 (1): 43–52.

———. 2012. "Land Reform in Africa: A Reappraisal." Brief 3, Rights to Resources in Crisis: Reviewing the Fate of Customary Tenure in Africa, Rights and Resources Initiative, Washington, DC, January.

Binswanger-Mkhize, H. P., C. Bourguignon, and R. van den Brink, eds. 2009. *Agricultural Land Redistribution: Toward Greater Consensus.* Washington, DC: World Bank.

Bruce, J., and S. E. Mighot-Adholla, eds. 1994. *Searching for Land Tenure Security in Africa*. Dubuque, IA: Kendall/Hunt Publishing.

Cotula, L., S. Vermeulen, R. Leonard, and J. Keeley. 2009. "Land Grab or Development Opportunity? Agricultural Investment and International Land Deals in Africa." International Institute for Environment and Development, London; FAO, Rome; International Fund for Agricultural Development, Rome.

Deininger, K. 2003. *Land Policies for Growth and Poverty Reduction*. World Bank Policy Research Report. Washington, DC: World Bank; New York: Oxford University Press.

Deininger, K., D. Byerlee, J. Lindsay, A. Norton, H. Selod, and M. Stickler. 2011. *Rising Global Interest in Farmland: Can It Yield Sustainable and Equitable Benefits?* Washington, DC: World Bank.

FAO (Food and Agriculture Organization of the United Nations). 2012. *Voluntary Guidelines on the Responsible Governance of Tenure of Land, Fisheries, and Forests in the Context of National Food Security*. Rome: FAO.

Kanyinga, K. 2009. "Land Redistribution in Kenya." In *Agricultural Land Redistribution: Toward Greater Consensus*, edited by H. P. Binswanger-Mkhize, C. Bourguignon, and R. van den Brink. Washington, DC: World Bank.

Place, F., and S. Mighot-Adholla. 1998. "Land Registration and Smallholder Farms in Kenya." *Land Economics* 74 (3): 360–73.

van den Brink, R., G. Thomas, H. Binswanger, J. Bruce, and F. Byamugisha. 2006. "Consensus, Confusion, and Controversy: Selected Land Reform Issues in Sub-Saharan Africa." Working Paper 71, World Bank, Washington, DC.

World Bank. 2005. *Doing Business in 2006: Creating Jobs* Washington, DC: World Bank.

———. 2011. *Doing Business 2012: Doing Business in a More Transparent World.* Washington, DC: World Bank.

Chapter 2

The Impact of Documenting Land Rights on Investment and Productivity

While virtually all countries in Sub-Saharan Africa have the legal framework in place to document land rights, only a small proportion (about 10 percent) of occupied rural land is registered.[1] Although many reasons have been advanced to explain this, two are most commonly cited. First, until very recently, the predominant customary land tenure system was secure enough in many rural areas to provide adequate incentives for community members to invest in their land (Bruce and Mighot-Adholla 1994); investments in land registration programs were not necessary. Second, for many years after independence, documenting land rights involved detailed surveying and mapping of land boundaries, which was appropriate for high-value land in urban areas but a high-cost option for most rural lands, which are typically of lower value. Within the last 10 years, however, African countries have been experimenting with more appropriate and lower-cost approaches to documenting land rights. This chapter reviews this new generation of approaches for documenting land rights and the subsequent impacts on investment and productivity.

Experiences with Registration of Communal Land Rights

In many African countries, where much land is still held in common and land values are relatively low, delimitation or demarcation of boundaries and registration of community land can be more cost-effective and appropriate than registration of individually owned land. Many countries have already made legal provisions to recognize customary tenure and communal land (Alden Wily 2012) and are in a position to embark on the more urgent task of registering communal lands. The allocation and management of individual plots can be left to community institutions, with the option to transition to more formal systems of registering individual land rights as the need arises.

In addition to the potential for covering larger areas quickly, communal land registration can focus on more time-consuming institutional requirements, such as (a) formulating by-laws to govern how communities interact with outsiders or resolve conflicts (Knight et al. 2012) and (b) enabling communities to enter into and honor agreements on land use with outsiders to benefit both parties. Moreover, if information obtained from the delimitation of boundaries and registration of communal land is properly kept and publicly accessible, the transaction costs of investors from outside the community will be significantly reduced and the transparency of transactions considerably enhanced. Combined with legal measures, this could reduce the neglect of existing rights that often accompanies land-related direct investment (Alden Wily 2010; Anseeuw et al. 2012). Similarly, recognizing community rights and delimiting relevant boundaries would aid international programs in their efforts to counter global warming. For example, carbon offset programs of reforestation require documentation of land rights to identify and secure the rights of tree plantation owners. This section reviews progress made by Ghana, Mozambique, and Tanzania in registering communal land rights. To derive lessons for African countries, it ends with a review of the experience of Mexico, one of the most successful countries to recognize and register communal rights.

Ghana

About five years ago, Ghana began to pilot the demarcation of communal or customary land (see box 2.1). Since communal land is held by traditional authorities and Ghana's constitution empowers them to hold land in trust for their subjects, the process of demarcating and registering land does not require community organization; it covers only the identification, adjudication, and survey of boundaries, followed by registration. To date, only 10 areas have been covered, at a high average cost of US$500–US$700 per kilometer (see table 2.1); costs are high largely because of delays in agreeing on boundaries and the need to clear dense vegetation before surveying the boundaries. Measures are being taken to reduce the costs by deploying alternative dispute resolution (ADR) mechanisms to help traditional authorities to agree on boundaries before surveyors are mobilized for fieldwork. Demarcation of boundaries is being scaled up with support from the World Bank (World Bank 2011c).

Mozambique

Soon after its Land Law was passed in 1997, Mozambique started delimiting and registering communal land, but less than 10 percent of its rural communities had been delimited as of 2010. Unlike Ghana and Tanzania, Mozambican communities have to be organized into formal entities and their lands delimited one at a time, a slow process that costs between US$2,000 and US$10,000 per community

---

BOX 2.1
_____

Legalizing and Registering Communal Rights in Ghana, Mozambique, and Tanzania

Since 2005, the Ghanaian government has used funding from the Land Administration Project to demarcate, map, and register Stool/Skin lands in the names of traditional authorities, as was advocated in the 1999 national land policy and is in line with Ghana's constitution (World Bank 2003, 2011c). Funding covered 10 areas (Anum, Asebu, Builsa, Dormaa, Ejisu, Gbawe, Juaben, Tamale, Tieve, and Wassa Amenfi) and started as a pilot; the second phase of the project is now scaling up this effort (World Bank 2011b). The average cost to demarcate boundaries was US$500 to US$700 per kilometer, but this has since been reduced significantly by deploying ADR techniques to help traditional authorities agree on boundaries before surveying is done.

Mozambique's mechanisms for dealing with and formalizing customary land rights are largely bound up in a legal process known as "community land delimitation." The Technical Annex (to the 1997 Land Law) defines delimitation as "identification of the boundaries of the areas occupied by local communities including the entry of the information into the National Land Cadastre." The process of delimitation clearly identifies both the community and the extent of the land it holds, but does not specify its boundaries; "sketch maps" with general boundaries are agreed upon with neighboring communities. As of early 2010, only 231 communities, representing less than 10 percent of Mozambican "rural communities," had been delimited and given certificates, and a further 92 were in the process of doing so. The cost per unit to delimit and certify a community is US$2,000–US$10,000. A recent review recommended shifting away from the present sporadic approach and toward systematic delimitation, methodical strengthening of the capacities of land administration services, and careful engagement of local institutional actors.

With support from the World Bank, the process of surveying and registering village lands in Tanzania was accelerated in line with the Village Land Act 1999, which empowered village authorities to determine the use of land and allocate it to households within the villages and to investors from outside village communities (World Bank 2005). As of early 2012, more than 11,000 out of about 12,000 villages had been surveyed, of which about 7,000 had been registered. The average cost of surveying and registration is US$500 per village. It is expected that all village lands will be surveyed and registered by June 2013.

Sources: For Ghana, adapted from World Bank 2012; for Mozambique, adapted from World Bank and FAO 2010; and for Tanzania, adapted from World Bank 2005.

(table 2.1). A recent review of Mozambique's delimitation program recommended a systematic process of organizing communities and delimiting land.

Tanzania

Sub-Saharan Africa's most advanced communal land registry program is in Tanzania, which has registered 60 percent of its communal lands. Tanzania's

Table 2.1 Unit Costs of Surveying Community Land Boundaries in Ghana, Mozambique, and Tanzania

Country	Traditional management regime	Ecological description of area	Method of survey	Cost
Ghana	Customary land administered by traditional authorities	Many areas with dense vegetation	Fixed-boundary survey, mainly using global positioning system (GPS) or total stations	US$500–US$700 per kilometer
Mozambique	Community land administered by communities	Considerable resources for organizing communities	General-boundary survey, using sketch maps	US$2,000–US$10,000 per community
Tanzania	Village land administered by village councils	Few areas with dense vegetation	Fixed-boundary survey, mainly using GPS	US$77 per kilometer

program is administered by village councils, which are responsible for land, among other administrative duties. The average cost of demarcating and registering village (communal) land is about US$500 per village, or US$77 per kilometer (table 2.1). Surveying and registering the remaining 40 percent of communal lands is planned for completion by June 2013. The commissioner of lands is responsible for registering village land, with a certificate of village land (CVL) granted to the village council. The village council has the power to allocate, manage, and register individual rights only after receiving a CVL. Registration of individual rights within villages has been very slow. Although registration of communal lands in Tanzania has been ongoing since 2001 when the Village Land Act regulations were issued, less than 200,000 land parcels (out of about 25 million) within villages have been demarcated and certificates of registration issued to their owners.

Lessons from Experience with Registration of Communal Land Rights

At least three lessons can be gleaned from these experiences. First, Ghana's experience shows that demarcation of communal land boundaries is not merely a technical surveying exercise, but a process that requires time and financial resources to resolve disputes and agree on boundaries before field-work begins (as in Mexico). Second, Mozambique's experience indicates that, even without a legal requirement for a detailed survey of boundaries, registration of communal lands can be a very slow process if community owners of land are not clearly defined, such as established traditional authorities (as in Ghana) or statutory ones (as in Tanzania), and if new formal entities have to be developed. Third, Tanzania's experience shows that registration of communal land needs to be followed up with resources to plan for communal and individual land use and to delineate common-property resources (such as grazing land).

Three key lessons relevant for African countries can also be drawn from Mexico's *ejido* reforms, implemented in the late 1990s, to recognize and register communal rights (see box 2.2). First, dissemination of key reform messages and assistance enabled the achievement of nearly full participation in a voluntary process, thereby enabling cost-effective implementation of the program and benefits (for example, availability of registry information), which would have been impossible to attain using a more demand-driven approach. Second, although significant resources were spent on mapping, dealing effectively with institutional aspects (such as assistance in resolving conflicts and setting up community institutions to manage resources transparently and flexibly to respond to local needs) was a critical precondition for successful mapping. Third, the full benefits from such an effort were achieved only because there was a critical mass of communities with land to be registered and a public registry that provided public access to information and updated spatial and textual information.

BOX 2.2

Legalizing and Registering Communal Rights in Mexico

Ejidos are communal settlements of land reform beneficiaries who received nontransferable use rights in a process that started in 1917 and reached its peak in the 1930s. The reforms were motivated to address three issues: (a) without land markets (and inheritance limited to only one heir), many old *ejidatarios* were unable to use their land efficiently and youth could not access land; (b) powerful members were able to appropriate large amounts of common-property resources for use as a source of patronage, hurting poor and indigenous people; and (c) urban expansion was based on informality, land invasions, and corruption rather than on planning. The need for action was accentuated by the fact that *ejidos* include 70 percent of Mexico's forestland and two-thirds of the land needed for urban expansion.

Reforms comprised legal changes, institutional reform, and a systematic program of land regularization called Procede. They aimed to empower communities to choose the property rights regime most suitable to their needs; increase transparency, tenure security, and investment through the issuance of landownership certificates; facilitate land transfers; reduce the cost of verifying land rights; and deal with a backlog of inherited land conflicts. To strengthen the self-governance of *ejidos*, the law mandated creation

(continued next page)

Box 2.2 (continued)

of an assembly, a vigilance committee, and a secretariat to ensure division of powers and internal checks and balances.

Three types of institutions were established to support the process. First, 42 tribunals and an appeals tribunal were created to resolve a large backlog of land conflicts in a way that encouraged out-of-court settlement and access by the poor. About 350,000 conflicts were resolved between 1992 and 1999. Second, a registry with delegations in each state was created to document rights to individual and collective land and to identify individuals empowered to make decisions on behalf of the *ejido*. Finally, the Office of the Ombudsman, with representation in each state, was created to provide paralegal assistance and oversight, to prevent elite capture, and to help small farmers assert their rights.

A program of voluntary land regularization clarifies property rights for individual *ejidos* in a 12- to 18-month process. The process starts with *boundary assessment, demarcation, and conflict resolution* entailing an independent review of any legal documents relating to the *ejido* to determine whether any ambiguities or conflicts need to be resolved. Once external boundaries are determined, the Office of the Ombudsman launches a dissemination campaign to explain the nature and procedures of the program; this culminates in a formal decision of the assembly (with a 50 percent quorum) about whether to participate in the program. In case of a positive decision, a committee of *ejidatarios* identifies the boundaries of different types of land (that is, urban plots, parcels, and common lands), prepares sketch maps, and establishes a complete inventory of rights, after pending conflicts have been resolved (or registered separately). A second assembly clears the way for formal demarcation of lands and a public display of the results for at least two weeks. A third assembly, with a quorum of at least 75 percent of all community members, a public notary, and a representative of the Office of the Ombudsman, clears the way for publishing results in the registry and distributing the certificates.

Procede's quantitative accomplishments are impressive. Within a five-year period, 57.2 million hectares of land were measured and mapped and 2.9 million households received certificates to individual, common, and housing land. The program increased security of land access for about 1 million households who previously had little or no rights to land. It also improved governance; more than 18,000 *ejidos* formalized internal by-laws through the assembly, and 90 percent elected representatives in a democratic process. The program was positively perceived by participants and improved household welfare by increasing participation in the nonagricultural economy. Contrary to initial fears, it did not cause a wave of land sales but instead provided a basis for numerous contracts and joint ventures. Although the costs were rather high due to the technology available at the time, they would have been a fraction of the cost paid if today's technology had been used. Even so, the net benefits were positive.

Source: Adapted from World Bank 2002.

Experience with Systematic Registration of Individual Land Rights in Sub-Saharan Africa

In recent years, Ethiopia and Rwanda have made tremendous progress in documenting land rights. Using a "general-boundary" approach to underpin a participatory community-based process, both countries were able to register land rights for a large number of land parcels in a relatively short time and at low cost. Other African countries, including Madagascar and Tanzania, are piloting a similar approach to registering individual land rights. This section outlines the progress made by these four countries, highlights key features of design and implementation, and shares some preliminary results. There is also a short discussion of pilots in Ghana and Uganda that use a similar systematic approach, but are based on detailed surveys of boundaries. While not yet fully evaluated, a new and promising approach to registering individual land rights through rural land use plans being piloted in West Africa is also reviewed, and lessons are drawn from its experience in design and implementation.

Ethiopia

Since the late 1990s, Ethiopia has awarded certificates for more than 25 million parcels in rural areas all over the country at a scale, pace, and cost-effectiveness unprecedented in Sub-Saharan Africa. Its homegrown process has been participatory and public. Regional governments in the four main regions (Amhara, Oromia, SNNPR [Southern Nations, Nationalities, and Peoples' Region], and Tigray) used basically the same approach and methodology but developed different formats for records and certificates. In a pragmatic approach, all four regional governments adopted a two-level certification process. First-level certification was achieved via locally elected committees that gathered information on landholdings, without using a spatial framework or map base, in a very short time frame. A land use and administration committee, elected by popular vote, assumed responsibility for a labor-intensive and field-based process whereby parcels were publicly registered. Once all information for a village had been entered into a registry book, an official certificate was issued to each parcel owner.

Using locally elected, unpaid community land use and administration committees and forgoing surveying of land boundaries kept costs at about US$3.50 per household (or about US$1.00 per parcel), even in Amhara, which had the most outside input. Despite the low cost, field evidence suggests that the process produced tangible benefits: reducing conflicts, empowering women, increasing individual and community investment, and improving security. However, issues linger with the first-level certification: documentation and registration forms are difficult to maintain, records are not always updated, and a spatial framework is lacking. While these issues were to be addressed in the second-level certification, as of mid-May 2012 that process had not been clearly defined. The government of Ethiopia and the four regional governments declared that second-level certification would be completed in five years, but a recent review of capacity in the four main regions indicated serious shortages in staffing and limited capability in all regions other than Amhara. Due to the country's large size and the immense investment costs, efforts are focused on finding the most appropriate mix of technologies to minimize costs without sacrificing survey accuracy.

Ghana

Systematic registration was piloted in periurban areas of Ghana from 2008 to 2010 based on detailed surveying of boundaries by private contractors, with funding from the World Bank (World Bank 2003). The pilot covered nearly 10,000 land parcels. The estimated cost was US$32 per title. A project funded by the Millennium Challenge Corporation around the same time produced a limited number of titles (351) at a cost of US$200–US$250 per title, but this cost (which was very high partly because of overhead costs, including those of a land office and a continuously operating reference station) is expected to decrease significantly as production expands. Ghana's systematic approach to registration is based on a legal framework that requires a detailed survey of boundaries and is appropriate only for high-value land in urban and semiurban or commercialized rural areas. In low-value rural areas, a general-boundary approach is more appropriate.

Madagascar

Launched in 2005 with multidonor support led by the Millennium Challenge Corporation, Madagascar's National Land Program set up a government entity to manage its land tenure reform. Key design features included modernization and computerization of land and surveying services, decentralization of land management, renewal of land laws and regulations, and training for decentralized land management. Implementation of the land tenure reform started by eliminating the colonial era principle that land is presumed to belong to the state, which cleared the way for recognizing individual land rights using a local procedure and local entities. Between 2006 and 2009, 400 out of 1,500 municipalities were equipped with a municipal land office, and a new legal framework enabled them to issue 75,000 certificates. These certificates have the same legal value as traditional land titles but are issued in a much shorter time and at lower cost, as they are based on satellite imagery or an aerial photomap. The average cost was US$14 per certificate and processing time was six months, an improvement over the previous system, which produced 2,000–3,000 land titles per year, involved 24 steps, took up to six years, and cost an estimated US$500 per title. Future pilots will address registration of secondary rights and introduce land

Ceremonial Handing Over of Title Certificates in Winneba Town, Ghana

Photo credit: ©Isaac Karikari, project coordinator, Land Administration Project, Phase 2, Ghana.

transaction taxes to go along with registration. In addition, there is a need to restructure the land sector to integrate traditional land administration services with the new decentralized system of land management.

Rwanda

Rwanda is one of the most densely populated countries in Africa, with a population of about 9.9 million distributed over 20,635 square kilometers (a density of about 479 persons per square kilometer). Rapid population growth and the 1994 genocide weakened traditional land allocation systems, historically based in part on customary law and in part on written law in the civil law tradition. In June 2004, the government adopted a national land policy and, following a period of public consultation, passed an Organic Land Law, which took effect on September 15, 2005. The main objectives of Rwanda's national land policy were to register all landownership in the country and rationalize land use. Toward this end, field consultations were undertaken in 2006, and subsequent field trials were conducted in four localities from late 2007 through 2008. A five-year plan was prepared to complete systematic registration from 2009 to 2013.

A key decision made in adopting the national land policy and passing the Organic Land Law was that a unified leasehold tenure system would be implemented via a systematic Land Tenure Regularization (LTR) Program across the whole country in a short time frame. In July 2008, Rwanda's government decided that land titling fieldwork would be completed in two years and titling in five. While the LTR Program is an initiative of the government of Rwanda, the U.K. Department for International Development provided the bulk of financial and technical support; several other development partners also provided support, including the European Community and the Swedish International Development Cooperation Agency.

The task was significant: the initial estimate of 7 million land parcels later increased to about 10.3 million land parcels, located in 30 districts and 416 sectors with more than 2,146 cells (the lowest administrative unit). The country has a very low institutional base and low capacity for land administration at all levels. The approach adopted in the pilots and in the subsequent scale-up was a systematic parcel-by-parcel and cell-by-cell participatory activity undertaken in close cooperation with cell land committees. Low-technology "general-boundary" rules and simple methods of boundary demarcation, designated by locally trained parasurveyors based on aerial photography and satellite imagery, were used. The estimated average costs per land parcel for the five-year program were about US$10, with estimated annual recurrent costs for updating of US$0.82 and US$0.90 per urban and rural parcels, respectively.

In June 2012, the LTR Program completed the demarcation and adjudication of the country's 10.3 million parcels of land; and it was on target to prepare and distribute 7 million leases to districts by the end of 2012. Leases are for 99 years for agricultural land categorized as individual land and for shorter periods for other uses and categories of land; they are collected by leaseholders upon payment of fees and signing of the lease agreement. As of the end of March 2012, nearly 1 million leases had been collected. A quarterly report (to March 2012) indicated that 7 percent of the claimants were women, 5 percent were men, 83 percent were married couples, and 1 percent consisted of other legal entities. In mid-2012, the LTR records were being prepared for transfer to a land administration information system, and district staff were being trained to record transactions. Several issues still need to be addressed, including the use of fees and charges and the need for a strategy to build districts' capacity to maintain and sustain the land information and registration systems, but Rwanda is on record to have demarcated all land parcels in the country by June 2012 and was on track to register and prepare leases for at least 83 percent of these parcels by the end of 2012, a significant achievement.

Tanzania

Under a project funded by the World Bank, a systematic adjudication pilot was undertaken in Babati and Bariadi districts to implement Tanzania's Village Land Act (World Bank 2005). In these two districts, 33,350 land parcels were adjudicated based on satellite imagery, and about 27,000 certificates of customary rights of occupancy (CCROs) were issued at an average cost of US$45 per parcel (or issued CCRO). The unit cost was higher than projected (US$22 per issued CCRO) largely because the level of output was lower and costs were higher than anticipated, the result of high field expenses incurred by staff from central and district offices. A more efficient procedure is planned for the scale-up by district staff, with a target unit cost of less than US$20 per issued CCRO. While in the upper range of comparable large-scale systematic registration activities (for example, about US$10 per parcel in Rwanda; US$25 per parcel in Thailand), this unit cost is still significantly lower than that of the traditional approach in Tanzania, whereby registered surveyors undertook accurate ground surveys in rural areas at a cost exceeding US$200 per parcel. The cost of issuing a CCRO also included the cost of participatory land use planning. Future costs will be reduced even further as forms and formats are modified, data held at district and village levels are rationalized, and the process is streamlined.

Uganda

Like Ghana, Uganda also conducted systematic registration pilots based on a fixed-boundary legal framework using ground survey methods, with funding provided by the World Bank (World Bank 2004). Undertaken in Iganga, Mbale, and Ntungamo districts and covering more than 10,000 land parcels, the pilots were informed by initial community baseline studies undertaken to gauge community expectations, followed by community sensitization programs. The land survey was undertaken by public surveyors, while adjudication included local area land committees. The pilots were successful in introducing a participatory and reduced-cost approach to registration, which resulted in an average cost of registration of US$23 per parcel, comparable to Thailand's US$25 per parcel. Uganda's registration approach, based on detailed surveying of boundaries, was appropriate for urban and periurban and rural commercial areas of high value, but not for low-value rural lands, which are more appropriately registered using a general-boundary approach based on a photomap.

Lessons from Recent Experience in Africa with the Systematic Registration of Individual Rights

The following key lessons can be drawn from the successful systematic registration activity in Ethiopia, Rwanda, and, to a lesser extent, Madagascar: (a) it is important to have strong political will for the activity; (b) the close involvement of local authorities—land use and allocation committees in Ethiopia, cell land committees in Rwanda, and municipal land offices in Madagascar—not only builds legitimacy for the process but is a key element in reducing the cost of systematic registration; and (c) the adoption of low-technology "general boundaries," rules, and simple methods implemented by paraprofessionals to demarcate and chart boundaries using image maps as a spatial framework is both feasible and cost-effective. While significant progress has been made to reduce the costs of registering individual land rights, there is a continued search for approaches to reduce registration costs even further. One of the promising approaches is the Social Tenure Domain Model (STDM), which aims to record undocumented customary land as well as other land and properties in informal settlements with a view to integrating the information captured into the mainstream land administration system. A prototype of the STDM has been produced and is being piloted with a view to moving it to full development (Lemmen 2010).

Registration of Individual Land Rights through PFRs in West Africa

Rural land use plans (*plans fonciers ruraux,* PFRs) are a tool used to improve land management and administration by offering a legal and institutional framework that secures local rights by documenting them and strengthens the role of local land management institutions.[2] PFRs are based on a village-level mapping approach that starts with field surveys to carify land use claims and delineate parcel boundaries in a consensual manner involving the owners or users of surveyed parcels and neighboring ones. This leads to the signing of minutes and creation of a map of the village showing all surveyed parcels as well as a registry of land users. The registry can include information on owners as well as on secondary-rights holders. The map is publicly displayed for several weeks to ensure that all counterclaims can be raised and addressed. Once rights have been clearly identified, agreed upon, and registered, a land use certificate is issued.

Benin, Burkina Faso, and Côte d'Ivoire have been piloting several forms of PFRs. Although it is too early to draw conclusive lessons, a review of the design and implementation of these pilots nevertheless provides useful insights for other African countries.

Benin   In Benin, insecurity of land tenure, perceived to be a consequence of oral agreements, has resulted in numerous conflicts. To address the issue, the government has been implementing two projects since 1993—the Projet de Gestion des Ressources Naturelles, funded by the World Bank, Agence Française de Développement (AFD), and German Technical Cooperation (GTZ), and the Projet de Gestion des Terroirs et des Ressources Naturelles, funded by AFD and GTZ. Based on the model of Côte d'Ivoire, PFRs were introduced as an incentive to promote rural land use planning; 41 pilots were established without envisioning the need to issue land rights documents. Based on Law 2007-03, subsequent PFRs were refocused so that landholders whose rights are confirmed through the PFR process receive a land certificate that legally confirms their individual or collective rights. This procedure allows the legal recognition of customary rights of individual households but not communal rights and sets up a local system of land administration.

In 2005 the Millennium Challenge Account (MCA) and the government of Benin started a project to modernize and standardize the legal framework, convert land use permits into titles in urban areas, and implement PFRs in rural areas. The project focused on standardizing the land tenure systems of both rural and urban areas to facilitate private investment by formalizing land rights and developing land markets. The goal was to simplify the procedures for registering property rights and to increase the registration of individual land rights and issuance of individual land titles. An agency, the Agence Nationale des Domaines et du Foncier, was to be created to manage the project. In urban areas, the program, which sought to transform a massive amount of land use permits (*permis d'habiter*) into land titles, produced only modest results. The rural component of the program was more effective, as 294 villages started a PFR (out of a target of 3,000). However, the process is not yet complete; at the end of 2011, when MCA closed its land activities, fewer than 1,000 certificates had been issued (out of a target of 75,000). But the design of PFRs underwent a fundamental change; originally intended as an alternative to traditional land titling, PFRs finally became a tool for its implementation. Despite the visions expressed in policy documents produced in parallel (*Livre Blanc 2009, Lettre de Cadrage 2009,* draft of the *Code Domanial et Foncier 2012*), a lack of consensus on the objectives and approach of PFRs remains, as do many fundamental questions. One is the ambiguity regarding the nature of the delivered rights and the tools to formalize them: Are the ultimate documents produced land use certificates or titles delivered through subsequent conversion of land certificates? Is the conversion of land certificates to titles compulsory or voluntary? Are recognized rights only individual (as implied by land rights documents), or could various local rights be registered in the process?

Institutional issues also need to be addressed. For example, it is not clear whether the current approach will be based on decentralization to the municipality level or on "deconcentration" from the future Agence Nationale du Domaine et du Foncier. At the moment, it is also not clear whether local governments are ready to manage the process; support to build the capacity of local governments is needed and should be planned. The current draft of the Land Code aims to merge the land title and the land certificate into a single certificate of individual landownership (*certificate de propriété foncière*). This is now being questioned, particularly in rural areas, as in many villages a significant amount of land is still held in common, including unshared inherited land and communal land reserves. An evaluation of the particularly rich experience of Benin would be timely to support the formulation of answers to these questions before PFRs are scaled up to the country's 3,000 villages.

Burkina Faso   Based on significant national discussions and several pilot operations, including the PFRs of Ganzourgou, the government of Burkina Faso approved a national policy for rural land in 2007 to provide the rural population with equitable access to land, secure their investment, and give them a mechanism for resolving land disputes. Earlier PFRs had been limited to local pilot operations for clarifying and recognizing individual land rights. This information was used to design the national policy for rural land and Law 034-2009 on rural land, whose key innovations were (a) recognizing landownership through a local procedure to issue a landownership certificate (*attestation de possession foncière*) and recognize land use rights as leases, rentals, or temporary authorizations to cultivate; (b) establishing local land management services, including rural services in charge of managing communal and individual land assets, village land commissions, and local land committees; and (c) recognizing local land agreements aiming to determine rules regarding management of common natural resources.

Burkina Faso's land policy reform is now being scaled up by implementing new land management bodies in the first 17 municipalities sponsored by the MCA. In addition, the MCA supported completion of Ganzourgou's PFRs, including the process of issuing landownership certificates. It is too early to draw lessons from these operations, as local land management services, although operational, are just starting to process the first applications for land certificates and collective land agreements are just being implemented. The government of Burkina Faso and its development partners plan to extend the implementation of Act 034-2009 provisions to 12 municipalities and gradually to equip all 350 communes of Burkina Faso with local land services.

Côte d'Ivoire   Based on a decision of its Council of Ministers in December 1988, Côte d'Ivoire was the first West African country to introduce PFRs, with the objective of identifying land for young farmers and using the experience to design an updated land policy. Beginning in 1990, the AFD supported implementation on a pilot basis in five areas of the country at a time when young farmers seeking land to cultivate were questioning former land agreements established with migrants. The PFRs seem to have exacerbated the conflict. On the one hand, indigenous people saw PFRs as an attempt to formalize land use rights acquired by "foreigners" (migrants and Ivorian individuals coming from the north) and as a risk to expropriation of their own land. On the other hand, migrants saw PFRs as a way to secure their land use rights permanently.

In 1997 the PFRs were scaled up with the support of Projet National de Gestion des Terroirs et d'Équipement Rural, funded by the World Bank, the AFD, and the government of Côte d'Ivoire, in four new areas, but implementation was disrupted by the civil war. Land issues may have added to the conflict; Law 98-750 on Rural Land, enacted to support the scale-up, tended to reserve the recognition of land rights for Ivorian nationals, which likely increased social tensions. The current period of reconciliation provides a favorable environment in which to revive the national debate for an updated land policy. An evaluation of the PFRs could inform this debate.

Lessons from piloting and implementing PFRs in West Africa   While several lessons can be drawn from the early experiences of PFRs in West Africa, two stand out. First, in Côte d'Ivoire, basing the PFR scale-up on a law on rural land escalated a land conflict into a civil war; the lesson is that PFRs should be preceded by a national policy to build consensus on nationally acceptable objectives, strategies, and approaches to designing and implementing PFRs, as was done in Burkina Faso. Second, Benin and Côte d'Ivoire, unlike Burkina Faso, enacted laws to implement PFRs that focused only on recognizing and documenting individual land rights; the lesson is that this should be done together with or preceded by legal provisions to recognize, delineate, and create institutions to manage common-property resources and to deal with conflicts among villages or communities, such as those between mobile pastoralists and settled farmers.

Impacts of Land Rights Documentation on Agricultural Investments and Productivity

Measuring the impact of land tenure security on agricultural production is a challenging task, although the positive relationship between the two has been clearly established theoretically and convincing empirical evidence of it has been identified in China, Eastern Europe, Latin America, and Thailand.[3] However, the impact is determined not only by tenure security, but also by factors in the economic environment in which land rights are formalized.[4] In addition, certain impacts take a long time to materialize. For example, the relationship between land tenure security and improved access to financial credit depends on the degree of maturity of rural financial markets, which could take a long time to develop. The complexity of the issue reinforces the argument that formalization of land rights should fit within a broader strategy of rural development, lest imperfections in some factor markets undermine the benefits from improved security.

Debate about the impact of land tenure security on agricultural production in Sub-Saharan Africa has undergone a long journey. During the 1970s and 1980s, the general consensus was that creating documentary evidence through title deeds was important for securing land tenure, which was necessary to support intensification of agriculture through enhanced investments and agricultural productivity (van den Brink et al. 2006). During the 1990s and thereafter, evidence indicated that a formal title was not always necessary or sufficient to provide strong tenure security (Deininger 2003). Many customary tenure systems in Africa were found to provide sufficient tenure security to stimulate investment and growth, although the main mechanism for transferring inherited property discriminated against women and migrants.[5] The backlash against the efficacy of land titling in Africa was, to a large extent, due to two factors: (a) land titling approaches were costly relative to their derived benefits, as they were based on detailed surveys of boundaries, even for rural lands of relatively low value, and (b) titles quickly went out of date, as registration costs were high and transfers were not always registered (Place and Mighot-Adholla 1998). In 2011, land registration costs in Sub-Saharan Africa, at 9.4 percent of property value, were more than double those in Organisation for Economic Co-operation and Development countries, at 4.4 percent of property value (World Bank 2011a).

But several recent events have made land registration a viable proposition in Africa. First, African countries are increasingly piloting and adopting less costly methods of land registration, mostly using photomaps to identify land boundaries; they are also issuing upgradable land rights documents in addition to full-title deeds (as in Rwanda). Second, they are increasingly reducing the cost of registering land transfers, by decentralizing and computerizing reengineered processes and workflows and reducing transaction taxes, primarily stamp duties. For example, as of 2010, both Ghana and Rwanda had reduced the cost of transferring property to less than 1 percent of property value (World Bank 2010). Third, the combination of increased foreign direct investment in African agriculture and higher population and economic growth has increased land values and demand for communal lands, making traditional landholders vulnerable to dispossession (Deininger et al. 2011). This has increased the return on investment in registering low-cost land to protect the rights of local landholders and to secure the access of investors to land. Preliminary but quite convincing evidence increasingly finds a positive relationship between tenure security and land-related investment. Against this background, the next sections review recent evidence of the impact of the new generation of low-cost methods of registering land on agricultural investment, productivity, and growth in Benin, Ethiopia, and Rwanda.

Benin

Benin's government started a PFR pilot that formalizes the land claims of agricultural households by recognizing customary arrangements in a participatory process at the village level. The approach consists of documenting land claims by consensually mapping all agricultural uses within a village, surveying the corresponding plots, and then handing out individual land use certificates to smallholders. Making use of a recent large-scale program of PFRs that randomly selected beneficiary villages through public village-level lotteries allows for a rigorous analysis of the program's effect (possibly disaggregated by gender) on a variety of dimensions such as tenure security, land market participation, and land investments. To carry out a state-of-the-art impact evaluation of the program, the World Bank collected data in nearly 300 program and comparison villages covering approximately 3,500 households. Analysis is under way, and results regarding the preliminary effects of the program should be available around January 2013 (Selod, personal communication, 2012).

Only short-term impacts are currently available given that these programs are still relatively new. The longer-term effects could be larger or smaller than the ones presented here, because they are affected by many other factors. However, it is clear that weak land rights in Sub-Saharan Africa, often held by disadvantaged groups such as women or outsiders, can undermine investment and reduce productivity (Deininger and Jin 2006; Fenske 2011; Goldstein and Udry 2008). Land rights security is related directly to the continent's food security, as recent studies show that no African country (except South Africa) achieves even 25 percent of its potential land productivity (Deininger, Ali, and Alemu 2011b). The investments needed to bridge this productivity gap are unlikely to be forthcoming without secure land rights.

Ethiopia

Based on data collected in 2007, a short-term impact evaluation of Ethiopia's land certification program using a difference-in-difference approach showed that the program significantly reduced the fear of land loss by about 10 percentage points. As a result of improved tenure security, the propensity to invest in soil and water conservation measures increased by 20–30 percentage points, and the number of hours spent on such activities increased significantly with program participation. Further analysis suggests that certification-induced investment increased output by about 9 percentage points (Deininger, Ali, and Alemu 2011a). With mean annual output equivalent to US$344 per hectare, benefits in the first year alone were US$5.80–US$9.10 per hectare, sufficient to cover the program's costs (US$3.20 per hectare).

Rwanda

The Rwandan government began implementing a land registration program in 2006. Based on a survey conducted in 2009, a short-term impact evaluation of the program using a geographic discontinuity design with spatial fixed effects found significant benefits. For example, landowners whose parcels were registered (particularly those in female-headed households) were more likely to invest in soil conservation measures (for example, bunds, terraces, or check dams) on their land. Registered households were more than twice as likely (10 percent) to invest than were those whose land was not registered. For female-headed households, the likelihood of investing was even higher, at 19 percentage points (Ali, Deininger, and Goldstein 2011).

Notes

1. This chapter considers registration of land as a process separate from registration of other land-related natural resources, such as minerals, water, and forests. Ownership of land and ownership of minerals underground are separate and are registered separately in most jurisdictions worldwide. Similarly, ownership of land and the water and forests on the surface tend to be separate in many jurisdictions, but not cleanly so. For water, the owner of land can also enjoy riparian rights, but the extent of enjoyment may depend on whether the water is tidal or navigable. The rights to water are registered separately from the rights to land in most global jurisdictions. Finally, ownership of land and rights to forests are often separated, but not cleanly. Rights to small and agro-forests tend to be bundled and registered with rights to land as individual or collective rights, while rights to forest reserves and large forests tend to be registered separately from land and owned by the state (in the case of forest reserves) or by the state or private commercial entities (in the case of large, unprotected forests).
2. This section draws generously from Chauveau, Bosc, and Pescay (1998); Chauveau (2003); Edja and Le Meur (2004); Jacob (2010); Koné (2006); Lavigne Delville (2006, 2010a, 2010b); Le Meur (2006, 2008); Ouédraogo (2005); Stamm (1999, 2000); and Thieba (2009). It also benefited from direct communication with Philippe Lavigne Delville regarding Benin and Pascal Thinon regarding Burkina Faso.
3. On the theory, see Deininger and Feder (2009). On China, see Jacoby, Li, and Rozelle (2002). On Eastern Europe, see Rozelle and Swinnen (2004). On Latin America, see Deininger and Chamorro (2004) and Fort (2007). On Thailand, see Feder et al. (1988).
4. These factors include maturity of financial markets in rural areas, access to markets for inputs and outputs, population density, agro-ecological potential, and farming systems.
5. On customary tenure systems, see Bruce and Mighot-Adholla (1994) and Platteau (1996). On discrimination against women, see Leonard and Toulmin (2000). On discrimination against migrants, see Cotula (2007).

References

Alden Wily, L. 2010. "Whose Land Are You Giving Away, Mr. President?" Paper presented at the Annual Conference "Land Policy and Land Administration," World Bank, Washington, DC, April 26–27.

————. 2012. "Land Reform in Africa: A Reappraisal." Brief 3, Rights to Resources in Crisis: Reviewing the Fate of Customary Tenure in Africa, Rights and Resources Initiative, Washington, DC, January.

Ali, D., K. Deininger, and M. Goldstein. 2011. "Environmental and Gender Impacts of Land Tenure Regularization in Africa: Pilot Evidence from Rwanda." Policy Research Working Paper 5765, World Bank, Washington, DC.

Anseeuw, W., L. Alden Wily, L. Cotula, and M. Taylor. 2012. "Land Rights and the Rush for Land: Findings of the Global Commercial Pressures on Land Research Project." International Land Coalition, Rome.

Bruce, J., and S. E. Mighot-Adholla, eds. 1994. *Searching for Land Tenure Security in Africa*. Dubuque, IA: Kendall/Hunt Publishing.

Chauveau, J.-P. 2003. "Plans fonciers ruraux: Conditions de pertinence des systèmes d'identification et d'enregistrement des droits coutumiers." Issue Paper 122, International Institute for Environment and Development, London.

Chauveau, J.-P., P.-M. Bosc, and M. Pescay. 1998. "Le plan foncier rural en Côte d'Ivoire." In *Quelles politiques foncières en Afrique rurale?* edited by Lavigne Delville. Paris: Ministère de la Coopération/Karthala.

Cotula, L. 2007. "Changes in Customary Land Tenure Systems in Africa." International Institute for Environment and Development, London.

Deininger, K. 2003. *Land Policies for Growth and Poverty Reduction*. World Bank Policy Research Report. Washington, DC: World Bank; New York: Oxford University Press.

Deininger, K., D. A. Ali, and T. Alemu. 2011a. "Impacts of Land Certification on Tenure Security, Investment, and Land Market Participation: Evidence from Ethiopia." *Land Economics* 87 (2): 312–34.

————. 2011b. "Productivity Effects of Land Rental Markets in Ethiopia: Evidence from a Matched Tenant-Landlord Sample." Policy Research Working Paper 5727, World Bank, Washington, DC.

Deininger, K., D. Byerlee, J. Lindsay, A. Norton, H. Selod, and M. Stickler. 2011. *Rising Global Interest in Farmland: Can It Yield Sustainable and Equitable Benefits?* Washington, DC: World Bank.

Deininger, K., and J. S. Chamorro. 2004. "Investment and Income Effects of Land Regularization: The Case of Nicaragua." *Agricultural Economics* 30 (2): 101–16.

Deininger, K., and G. Feder. 2009. "Land Registration, Governance, and Development: Evidence and Implications for Policy." *World Bank Research Observer* 24 (2): 233–66.

Deininger, K., and S. Jin. 2006. "Tenure Security and Land-Related Investment: Evidence from Ethiopia." *European Economic Review* 50 (5): 1245–77.

Edja, H., and P.-Y Le Meur. 2004. "Le plan foncier rural au Bénin: Production de savoir, gouvernance et participation." IRD/Gret Document de Travail UR095-9, IRD-UR Régulations Foncières, Montpellier, France.

Feder, G., Y. Chalamwong, T. Onchan, and C. Hongladarom. 1988. *Land Policies and Farm Productivity in Thailand*. Baltimore, MD: Johns Hopkins University Press.

Fenske, J. 2011. "Land Tenure and Investment Incentives: Evidence from West Africa." *Journal of Development Economics* 95 (1): 137–56.

Fort, R. 2007. *Property Rights after Market Liberalization Reforms: Land Titling and Investments in Rural Peru.* Wageningen, Netherlands: University of Wageningen.

Goldstein, M., and C. Udry. 2008. "The Profits of Power: Land Rights and Agricultural Investment in Ghana." *Journal of Political Economy* 116 (6): 980–1022.

Jacob, J.-P. 2010. "Une brousse connue ne peut pas bouffer un fils de la terre! Droits sur la terre et sociologie du développement dans le cadre d'une opération de sécurisation foncière (Ganzourgou, Burkina Faso)." In *Les politiques d'enregistrement des droits fonciers: Du cadre légal aux pratiques locales*, edited by J.-P. Colin, P.-Y. Le Meur, and E. Léonard. Paris: L'Institut de Recherche pour le Développement.

Jacoby, H. G., G. Li, and S. Rozelle. 2002. "Hazards of Expropriation: Tenure Insecurity and Investment in Rural China." *American Economic Review* 92 (5): 1420–47.

Knight, R., J. Adoko, S. Siakor, A. Salomao, T. Eilu, A. Kaba, and I. Tankar. 2012. "The Community Land Titling Initiative: International Report." International Development Law Organization, Rome.

Koné, M. 2006. "Quelles lois pour résoudre les problèmes liés au foncier en Côte d'Ivoire?" *Grain de Sel* 36 (September–November): 1–4. Inter-Réseaux Développement Rural.

Lavigne Delville, P. 2006. "Registering and Administering Customary Land Rights: PFRs in West Africa." Presented at the conference, "Land Policies and Legal Empowerment of the Poor," World Bank, Washington, DC, November 2–3.

———. 2010a. "Competing Conceptions of Customary Land Rights Registration (Rural Land Maps PFRs in Benin): Methodological, Policy, and Polity Issues." Presented at the Annual Conference, "Land Policy and Land Administration," World Bank, Washington, DC, April 26–27.

———. 2010b. "Faisceaux de droits et opérations d'enregistrement foncier: Questionnements pour une étude d'impact des plans fonciers ruraux au Bénin." Rapport d'études, Gret.

Le Meur, P.-Y. 2006. "Governing Land, Translating Rights: The Rural Land Plan in Benin." In *Development Brokers and Translators*, edited by D. Lewis and D. Mosse. New York: Palgrave MacMillan.

———. 2008. "L'information foncière, bien commun et ressource stratégique: Le cas du Bénin." Issue Paper 147, International Institute for Environment and Development, London.

Lemmen, C. 2010. "The Social Tenure Domain Model: A Pro-Poor Land Tool." FIG Publication 52, International Federation of Surveyors, Copenhagen.

Leonard, R., and C. Toulmin. 2000. "Women and Land Tenure: A Review of the Issues and Challenges in Africa." International Institute for Environment and Development, Drylands Programme, London.

Ouédraogo, H. 2005. "Etude comparative de la mise en œuvre des plans fonciers ruraux en Afrique del'Ouest: Bénin, Burkina-Faso, Côte d'Ivoire." Etudes Juridiques en Ligne, FAO, Rome.

Place, F., and S. Mighot-Adholla. 1998. "Land Registration and Smallholder Farms in Kenya." *Land Economics* 74 (3): 360–73.

Platteau, J. P. 1996. "The Evolutionary Theory of Land Rights as Applied in Sub-Saharan Africa: A Critical Assessment." *Development and Change* 27 (1): 29–86.

Rozelle, S., and J. F. M. Swinnen. 2004. "Success and Failure of Reform: Insights from the Transition of Agriculture." *Journal of Economic Literature* 42 (2): 404–56.

Stamm, V. 1999. "The Rural Land Plan: An Innovative Approach from Côte d'Ivoire." GTZ, Bonn.

———. 2000. "Plan foncier rural en Côte d'Ivoire." Issue Paper 91, International Institute for Environment and Development, London.

Thieba, D. 2009. "Evaluation retrospective du plan foncier rural du Ganzourgou." GRE-FCO, Ouagadougou.

van den Brink, R., G. Thomas, H. Binswanger, J. Bruce, and F. Byamugisha. 2006. "Consensus, Confusion, and Controversy: Selected Land Reform Issues in Sub-Saharan Africa." Working Paper 71, World Bank, Washington, DC.

World Bank. 2002. "Mexico Land Policy: A Decade after the Ejido Reforms." Rural Development and Natural Resources Sector Unit, World Bank, Washington, DC.

———. 2003. "Ghana Land Administration Project." Project Appraisal Document, World Bank, Washington, DC.

———. 2004. "Uganda Second Private Sector Competitiveness Project." Project Appraisal Document, World Bank, Washington, DC.

———. 2005. "Tanzania Private Sector Competitiveness Project." Project Appraisal Document, World Bank, Washington, DC.

———. 2010. *Doing Business 2011: Making a Difference for Entrepreneurs.* Washington, DC: World Bank.

———. 2011a. *Doing Business 2012: Doing Business in a More Transparent World.* Washington, DC: World Bank.

———. 2011b. "Ghana Land Administration Project." Implementation Completion and Results Report, World Bank, Washington, DC.

———. 2011c. "Ghana Second Land Administration Project." Project Appraisal Document, World Bank, Washington, DC.

———. 2012. "Ghana Commercial Agricultural Project." Project Appraisal Document, World Bank, Washington, DC.

World Bank and FAO (Food and Agriculture Organization of the United Nations). 2010. "Mozambique Community Land Delimitation and Local Development." Policy Note, World Bank, Washington, DC; FAO, Rome.

Land Reforms for Reducing Poverty in Rural and Urban Areas

Chapter 3 reviews land reforms for reducing poverty in rural and urban areas, with a focus on four reforms for increasing access to land for poor and vulnerable groups in society:

- Redistributing unused and underused agricultural land to the landless and land poor to increase their productivity and income

- Regularizing land tenure for squatters in urban informal settlements to promote investment in occupied lands and improve the living conditions of occupants through better housing and upgraded infrastructure and other services

- Promoting rental markets for agricultural land to provide access to land for people who need more land and can use it more efficiently than the owners, while enabling landowners to keep their land, rent it out, and earn income

- Enhancing women's access to land through legal empowerment and land documentation procedures that allow women to own land singly or jointly with their spouses.

Experiences with Redistributing Agricultural Land

Land reforms and redistribution have been implemented in many countries with the aim of redistributing land to the landless and land-poor segments of the population. While there is a general consensus on the need to redistribute land, there is often controversy about how to do so peacefully and legally, without invoking rampant corruption, political interference, rent seeking, or social conflict (Binswanger-Mkhize, Bourguignon, and van den Brink 2009). Malawi's and South Africa's experiences with redistributive land reforms using a "willing-seller willing-buyer" (WSWB) approach offer constructive lessons, both good and bad, for other African countries. This section examines the programs in these two countries to highlight the positive impacts accruing to beneficiaries in the form of productivity, income, and food security gains and draws important lessons for the design and implementation of similar interventions in other countries. Box 3.1 provides an overview of both programs.

Malawi's pilot community-based rural land development project (begun in 2004) uses a transparent, voluntary, legal, and resource-supported approach to land redistribution. The pilot was meant to inform the design and subsequent implementation of a broader program of land reform (World Bank 2004b) and was modeled on Brazil's market-based approach.[1]

BOX 3.1

Redistributing Agricultural Land in Malawi and South Africa

To address the highly unequal distribution of overcrowded arable land, which coexists with underused large-scale farms, Malawi piloted a land reform program with funding from the World Bank (World Bank 2004b). The pilot project aimed to increase the income of about 15,000 rural poor families using a decentralized, community-based, and voluntary approach in four districts. Modeled on Brazil's market-based approach to land reform (under implementation since the mid-1990s), the pilot had three key elements: (a) voluntary acquisition by communities of land sold by willing estate owners; (b) resettlement and on-farm development, including transportation of settlers, establishment of shelter, and purchase of basic inputs and advisory services; and (c) survey and registration of redistributed land. Land reform beneficiaries, organized in voluntary groups, were self-selected on the basis of predefined eligibility criteria. Each family received a grant of US$1,050, managed directly by beneficiaries, with up to 30 percent for land acquisition and the rest for transportation, water, shelter, and farm development. Land for the project was acquired from willing sellers, the government, or private donations and was registered initially under group title; it is expected that individual titles will be provided to beneficiaries upon demand in the future. Implementation was decentralized through District Assembly institutions and required capacity enhancement, especially for surveying and registration (additional financing was approved by the World Bank in 2009).

Lessons learned from the pilot were expected to guide implementation of a broader program of land reform initially designed in 2004, but this is currently being revised. According to the impact evaluation, the project achieved even better results than the Brazilian model on which it was based (World Bank 2009): more than 1.5 hectares of land were distributed, on average, to each of 15,142 rural households (40,102 households in Brazil); agricultural incomes increased an average of 40 percent per year for beneficiaries (compared to nonbeneficiaries) between 2005–06 and 2008–09 (6 percent in Brazil); the economic rate of return was 20 percent (13 percent in Brazil); and impacts on the livelihoods of beneficiaries and surrounding communities were positive, with improvements in landholdings, land tenure security, crop production, productivity, income, and food security (similar results in Brazil).

(continued next page)

Box 3.1 (continued)

In South Africa, the new government that came into power at the end of apart-heid in 1994 introduced land reforms with three components: tenure reform, restitu-tion, and redistribution. From 1994 to 2000, under the redistribution component, a Settlement/Land Acquisition Grant (SLAG) of R 16,000 was allocated to beneficiary families with incomes below R 1,500 per month. In 2001 the SLAG was replaced by the Land Redistribution for Agricultural Development Program, with grants ranging from R 20,000 to R 100,000 given on a sliding scale corresponding to beneficiary con-tributions of at least R 2,500; these were given to individuals, rather than households, with no income eligibility criteria. Due to a law restricting the subdivision of land, beneficiaries wanting to acquire and operate large farms had to form groups, essen-tially becoming absentee landlords with contracted farm managers. Due to these pecu-liarities and other program constraints, implementation was slow and ineffective. As of March 2011, only 6.27 million hectares, representing 7.2 percent of land owned by white African farmers, had been redistributed to black African farmers, with minimal impact on beneficiaries' livelihoods. This is far from the goal of 30 percent redistribu-tion by 2014.

Source: For Malawi, adapted from Tchale 2012; for South Africa, adapted from Lahiff and Li 2012.

The project exceeded its original targets, and an impact evaluation found that more than 15,140 households were relocated to more than 35,000 hectares within five years.[2] On average, each household has more than 1.5 hectares on which to cultivate various food and cash crops. More than 95 percent of the beneficiary groups received title deeds for the land they acquired, enhancing their land tenure security. Malawi's land redistribution led to significant posi-tive impacts on the livelihoods of beneficiaries, as shown in table 3.1. Improve-ments were reported in landholdings, land tenure security, crop production, and productivity, with positive impacts on income and food security. The positive impacts are attributed to meticulous attention to design details during implementation, initial farm development support provided to farmers, and high fertility of the land acquired.[3] A financial and economic analysis confirmed that the program was financially and economically viable; the financial and eco-nomic rates of return were above the 12 percent threshold, with the economic rate of return estimated at 20 percent (Simtowe, Mangisoni, and Mendola 2011).

Malawi's pilot offers six lessons for any country contemplating redistributive land reforms:

- Community-driven land redistribution programs are possible and can be economically viable in Sub-Saharan Africa.
- Beneficiaries prefer to relocate within or close to their original homes, primarily to preserve their cultural and social ties.

Table 3.1 Impacts of Malawi's Pilot Community-Based Rural Land Development Project, 2005–09

Indicator	2005–06	2006–07	2007–08	2008–09
Project beneficiaries				
Landholding (hectares)	1.02	1.81	1.76	1.79
	(0.93)	(0.68)	(0.69)	(0.72)
Maize productivity (kilograms per hectare)	1,536	2,476	1,446	1,464
	(1,176)	(6,543)	(1,200)	(1,448)
Food security (months)	6.16	10.6	8.53	8.92
	(3.93)	(3.21)	(3.49)	(3.55)
Agricultural income (Malawi kwacha)	11,527	31,141	29,173	44,683
	(38,914)	(80,130)	(57,347)	(87,720)
Nonbeneficiaries				
Landholding (hectares)	0.88	0.92	0.91	0.95
	(0.62)	(0.64)	(0.69)	(0.76)
Maize productivity (kilograms per hectare)	1,268	1,309	1,206	1,474
	(995)	(1,140)	(885)	(1,519)
Food security (months)	7.74	8.56	7.44	8.89
	(3.72)	(3.79)	(3.70)	(3.70)
Agricultural income (Malawi kwacha)	4,620	6,089	6,666	10,616
	(18,291)	(17,167)	(22,627)	(21,412)

Source: Simtowe, Mangisoni, and Mendola 2011.
Note: Standard deviations are in parentheses.

- Capping the maximum amount of the beneficiary grant that can be spent to acquire land, but allowing flexibility to spend grant money on resettlement and land or farm development, encourages beneficiaries to seek and negotiate for lower-priced land.

- The market-assisted WSWB approach may not work if there are no taxes (ground rent) on land, if taxes are very low or poorly enforced, or if large-scale agriculture is subsidized through freehold land, as in Malawi. It is therefore necessary to precede or accompany land reform with a land tax on unused land, to improve the capacity and enforcement of tax (ground rent) collection, and to remove subsidies for large-scale farms, as Brazil did successfully in the 1980s and 1990s (World Bank 2009).

- Institutional capacity in land administration is critical for successful implementation of such projects, as evidenced by Malawi's need to seek additional financing.

- Land reform programs should be embedded within broader programs of rural development to ensure that beneficiaries are able to optimize the benefits of such programs.

South Africa's multifaceted program of land reform was designed to redress imbalances in landholding and to secure land rights for historically disadvantaged people. South Africa's constitution establishes the legal basis for land reform, particularly in its Bill of Rights, which places a clear responsibility on the state: "The public interest includes the nation's commitment to land reform and to reforms to bring about equitable access to all South Africa's natural resources" (sec. 25, 4). The constitution allows the state to expropriate property for a public purpose or in the public interest, subject to just and equitable compensation. The framework for land reform policy was clarified in the 1997 "White Paper on South African Land Policy" (Government of South Africa 1997); a draft Green Paper released in 2011 captures revisions that have been under discussion for many years (Government of South Africa 2011, sec. 6).

However, land reform in South Africa has fallen consistently behind the state's targets and popular expectations. While South Africa's initial goal in 1994 was to transfer 30 percent of its land within 5 years, the target period was first extended to 20 years and then another 10 years, to 2025. By March 2011, 6.27 million hectares had been transferred, constituting 7.2 percent of the total land to be transferred. The program has had a mixed effect on productivity and food security. Velente (2009) found no significant difference in food security and poverty status between program beneficiaries and nonbeneficiaries, while Van Royen (2009) found different effects on productivity depending on the initial characteristics and endowments of beneficiaries. The government has tended to attribute the slow progress and mixed results to resistance from landowners and the high price of land,[4] but independent studies point to a wider range of factors, including complex application procedures and bureaucratic inefficiency (Hall 2003). Major budgetary shortfalls for restitution from 2008 to 2010 and growing concerns about the collapse of production on land acquired under both restitution and redistribution have shifted policy away from acquisition and toward the productive use of land.

A recent review of South Africa's land reform program concluded that two important aspects are missing (Lahiff and Li 2012). First, there is no viable small-farmer path to development, which could enable the millions of households residing in communal areas and on commercial farms to expand their own production and accumulate wealth and resources in an incremental manner. This requires a radical restructuring of existing farm units to create family-size farms, more realistic farm planning, appropriate support from a much-reformed state agricultural service, and a much greater role for beneficiaries in the design and implementation of their own projects. Second, there is no sustained focus on implementation, resource mobilization, and timely policy adjustment. Nonetheless, the South African program offers six lessons for program design and implementation:

- Market-based reform alone does not work. The WSWB approach applied in South Africa since 1994 has clearly presented some challenges. As such, market purchases from willing sellers must be supported by genuinely pro-active interventions by the state to remove incentives for large holdings and to tax unused land above a certain threshold to enable beneficiaries to purchase land at normal market prices. An additional measure to facilitate the land market would be last-resort expropriation of land from unwilling sellers whose holdings exceed a legally mandated maximum size, following Brazil's model.

- Appropriate legislation and its rigorous application are needed, as are specific provisions on the rights and obligations of various parties, including the state, property owners, and potential beneficiaries. For example, legislative action is required to remove legal restrictions on the subdivision of land, which prevent large-scale farmland from being divided to suit the farming needs of land reform beneficiaries.

- There is a need to emphasize and promote more productive uses of land.

- Strengthening the capacity of state agencies is critical, especially for those involved in the acquisition and transfer of land, farm planning, and post-settlement support activities of the redistribution program.

- Civil society needs to be involved in sensitizing and improving the bargaining capacity of beneficiaries.

- Postsettlement support is critical to ensure the long-term success of land redistribution programs. A land reform program driven by markets alone is unlikely to reach or benefit the poor.

Experiences with Regularizing Land Tenure in Urban Informal Settlements

About half of the world's population of 7 billion (as of October 31, 2011) live in cities (UNFPA 2011). In Africa, 40 percent of the population live in cities, but 70 percent of those are in slum areas with poor living conditions, such as insecure access to land, water, sanitation, and durable or less-crowded housing. More than 5 million Kenyans live in urban slums in informal settlements (United Republic of Kenya n.d.); among the 1 million persons who live in Nairobi's slums, 73 percent fall below the poverty line and 92 percent are tenants (World Bank 2006; Gulyani, Talukdar, and Jack 2010). About 30 percent of Tanzania's population live in cities (as of 2010), with about 50–70 percent of the urban population living in slums in informal settlements (United Republic of Tanzania 2011). The fast growth in urbanization and slum populations in Sub-Saharan Africa offers challenges for reducing poverty but also opportunities to boost economic growth and improve services, taking advantage of the high population densities in urban and slum areas (World Bank 2008).

Since the 1960s, when African governments embarked on failed programs to clear and replace squatter settlements with low-cost housing (including Tanzania's Sites and Services and Squatter Upgrading Program), numerous global initiatives have sought to guide country-level interventions to improve living conditions in informal settlements. They include the Rio Declaration on Environmental Sustainability 1992; the United Nations Conference on Human Settlements (Habitat II) held in Istanbul in 1996, which adopted the Habitat Agenda focusing on sustainable development and adequate shelter; the Johannesburg Declaration of Implementation Targets of Adequate Shelter for All and Sustainable Human Settlements Development; and the United Nations Millennium Development Goals, specifically Goal 7, which seeks to ensure environmental sustainability by aiming, among other things, to halve by 2015 the proportion of people without sustainable access to safe drinking water and basic sanitation (Target 3) and to improve significantly the lives of at least 100 million slum dwellers by 2020 (Target 4; UN-Habitat 2003). But country-level implementation has lagged and in Sub-Saharan Africa has focused primarily on upgrading infrastructure and services, neglecting regularization of land tenure or relegating it to pilots.

More recently, countries have moved toward adopting an integrated approach and to scaling up land tenure regularization pilots (see box 3.2). For example, Kenya has taken policy and constitutional measures to establish a firm legal framework for regularizing tenure security in informal settlements and has embarked on a large multidonor-funded program to implement an integrated program regularizing land tenure and upgrading infrastructure in informal settlements in its 15 largest municipalities. Similarly, Tanzania has developed a legal framework and prepared, with World Bank support, a 10-year National Program for Regularization and Prevention of Unplanned Settlements, which takes an integrated approach to scaling up past efforts. Lesotho has developed the necessary legal framework and, with funding from the Millennium Challenge Corporation (MCC), is implementing land tenure regularization in Maseru (MCC 2011). In Sub-Saharan Africa, the emerging approach of land tenure regularization has six major elements: community education and participation on rights and responsibilities; adjudication and enumeration of rights of individuals and groups; agreement on and survey of land boundaries; physical planning with wide community participation; adjustment of boundaries, walls, fences, and buildings to meet the agreed physical plan; and recognition of land rights in a local or central formal system or in a local informal or semiformal system.

In addition, as part of implementing land tenure regularization, linkages have been created with other programs to ensure greater effectiveness and sustainable improvement. The more important of these include revenue generation based on improved land information, land tenure security, and living

BOX 3.2

Land Tenure Regularization Experiences in Kenya, Lesotho, and Tanzania

More than 5 million Kenyans live in urban informal settlements. After interventions to replace slums with low-cost housing from the 1960s to the 1980s, Kenya adopted a 15-year Slum Upgrading Program to provide community organization and mobilization, urban planning and development, tenure and residential security, and infrastructure services. Land tenure regularization interventions started in the 1970s, but regularization interventions through settlement schemes have tended to be unique. Up until 2011, limited pilot regularization schemes had been initiated in virtually all provinces, primarily on government land, but only about 30,000 titles had been issued. In December 2009, Kenya's Parliament approved a new national land policy (incorporated in a new constitution approved in August 2010), which states that the government shall (a) facilitate the regularization of existing squatter settlements found on public land for purposes of upgrading or development, (b) develop a slum upgrading and resettlement program under specified flexible tenure systems, and (c) prevent further slum development (Attorney General of Kenya 2010; United Republic of Kenya 2009). In 2011 a US$165 million project was initiated to improve living conditions in existing informal settlements by investing in infrastructure, strengthening tenure security, and planning for future urban growth to prevent the emergence of new slums (World Bank 2011a). Upgrading is undertaken only in slums where land tenure has been regularized to avoid benefits from accruing to landlords at the expense of squatters. Regularization comprises community education and participation on rights and responsibilities; adjudication and enumeration of individual and group rights; agreement on and survey of land boundaries; physical planning with wide community participation; adjustment of boundaries, walls, fences, and buildings to meet the agreed physical plan; and documentation of land rights, through allotment letters and title registration for groups or individuals.

In Lesotho, only 35 percent (in 2005) of the urban population live in slums, where owners are usually also the occupants, owners have semiformal documents, and there is less pressure on land than in many other African countries. Nevertheless, Lesotho has taken important steps to check the growth of urban informal settlements. In 2006, with assistance from MCC, Lesotho allocated US$20 million to improve land administration, including the regularization of land tenure (MCC 2011). A new Land Bill and an Institutional Reform Bill were passed in June 2010. A pilot land regularization project completed in 2011 in urban areas of Maseru led to the systematic regularization of some 4,000 leases. A second contract (starting in 2012) was for the issuance of 50,000 registered leases using procedures developed by the pilot, with one major exception: the high unit costs of the pilot were reduced by using graphical cadastral techniques rather than global positioning system (GPS) ground surveys. Where little detail distinguishes the landscape or nonpermanent structures mark boundaries, issues may arise

(continued next page)

Box 3.2 (continued)

in the future and should be considered. The tenure regularization process includes formalizing land tenure and adjusting boundaries to conform to standard right-of-access plans as well as identifying any unsafe areas, although no resettlement has yet been needed. The future challenges are to ensure that urban authorities establish and maintain services; urban planners work to prevent formal settlements from deteriorating into high-density slums; and the Land Administration Authority collects ground rents and local authorities collect property taxes.

In Tanzania, an estimated 30 percent of the population live in cities (as of 2010), with about 50–70 percent in slums in informal settlements (United Republic of Tanzania 2011). In 1962 the government embarked on the Slum and Squatter Clearance Program and established the National Housing Corporation to address problems regarding shelter in urban areas. In 1972, the government initiated the Sites and Services and Squatter Upgrading Program to provide serviced housing plots (United Republic of Tanzania 1972); in 1973, the Tanzania Housing Bank was established to provide housing loans to low-income households. Infrastructure upgrading in slums was supported by donors, including the World Bank (World Bank 2004a). Following the 1995 national land policy, the government developed a supportive legal framework for regularizing tenure and piloted it in Dar es Salaam and Mwanza, with World Bank funding (World Bank 2005); beneficiaries received certificates of rights of occupancy (CROs), which are essentially long-term leases. A comprehensive property registry of residents in unplanned settlements in Dar es Salaam had registered 230,000 properties as of 2006; of those, 95,000 informal occupants were issued residential licenses (a derivative right to occupy land) for up to five years. Based on the pilot, a 10-year National Program for Regularization and Prevention of Unplanned Settlements (2012–21) to upgrade slums and regularize land tenure, similar to Kenya's program, was submitted to the World Bank.

Source: Lloyd 2012.

conditions; provision of basic services; institutional reform to maintain the system of land rights in the future and to provide greater responsiveness to the public; and disaster risk management.

While implementation of land tenure regularization in Sub-Saharan Africa is still too new to offer lessons, preliminary results, especially in Lesotho and Tanzania, are encouraging. Furthermore, empirical evidence indicates that regularizing land tenure has a significant impact on investment, although the bulk of the research is outside Africa. For example, impact studies in Buenos Aires found that regularized squatters had a 40 percent higher probability of living in shelters with good walls or in good-quality housing (Galiani and Schargrodsky 2005). In Peru, rates of home renovation increased more than two-thirds above baseline levels, although most of the increase was financed out of pocket rather than through credit (Field 2005). In the Philippines, a comparison of housing prices in formal residential areas and informal areas of the city of Davao revealed that prices were 58 percent higher in formal areas than in informal ones, while rents were 18 percent higher; in Jakarta, registered land was up to 73 percent more valuable than similar land held by a weak claim (Friedman, Jimenez, and Mayo 1988). Within Africa, a recent study in Dar es Salaam, Tanzania, found that, although willingness (and ability) to pay for formal documentation of property rights remains well below the costs involved in current sporadic efforts to provide CROs (with lease durations from 33 to 99 years), it is much higher than current charges for issuing residential licenses—derivative land rights documents valid for up to 5 years that are inheritable but not transferable (Ali et al. 2012). Tanzania's results indicate that formal documentation of property rights (issuing CROs) using the more cost-effective systematic approach would be worth undertaking, as it would be affordable and costs would be lower than the expected benefits.

Reforming Land Rental Markets to Provide Land Access to the Poor and Promote Transformational Growth

Land rental markets are a low-cost mechanism, requiring limited capital expenditure, to transfer land to the landless, the land poor, migrants, and young farmers; to provide them with an opportunity to learn, practice, or strengthen their skills in farming; and to help them move up the ladder toward landownership. Land rental markets have a long history in West Africa and have often provided a means to access land for commercial production, such as for cocoa farming in Ghana, and to equalize farming operations (Amanor and Diderutuah 2001; Estudillo, Quisumbing, and Otsuka 2001). Evidence from Sudan indicates that land rental markets transfer land to smaller producers, while case studies across Sub-Saharan Africa suggest that land rental markets have a positive impact on equity, benefiting the poor and women (Kevane 1996; Place 2002). Land rental markets also can enhance efficiency by transferring land from less to more productive users at low cost. In China, rental activity contributed to occupational diversification and increased productivity by about 60 percent, one-third of which accrued to landlords and two-thirds to tenants (Deininger and Jin 2009). In Vietnam, both rental and sales markets were found to have a positive impact on productivity (Deininger and Jin 2003).

Land rental markets are also important in driving labor mobility and enhancing the structural transformation of economies. For example, during the 1980s and 1990s, hundreds of millions of people migrated from agricultural to nonagricultural areas of China and Vietnam, associated with the transformation of their nonfarm economies. While this migration was driven by economic opportunities outside agriculture, there is evidence that it was facilitated by the emergence or strengthening of land rental and sales markets, underpinned by institutional strengthening of land rights. In rural China, more secure land tenure permitted existing landowners to rent their land to others and to migrate to the booming coastal areas and cities where wages were more attractive. The share of migrants in the labor force increased from 5 percent in 1988 to 17 percent in 2000, or a total of 124.6 million people; that figure is expected to reach 200 million by 2020 (Zhai, Hertel, and Wang 2003; Deininger and Jin 2007). The rapid migration led to a structural transformation of the economy, with the share of agriculture in total employment declining from 70 percent in 1978 to 50 percent by 2000 (Johnson 2000). Sub-Saharan Africa has experienced high economic growth over the last five years; if economic growth is to continue, it is important for labor to be mobile to meet demand.

At least two factors are critical for land rental markets to provide access to land for those who need and can use it best, to enhance productivity and incomes, and to enhance structural transformation of African economies. The first factor is making land tenure more secure. There is enough evidence that improved land rights, through the introduction of long-term leases or certification of land rights, have increased land rental activity in various countries, including China, the Dominican Republic, Ethiopia, Nicaragua, and Vietnam (Deininger and Feder 2009). In Sub-Saharan Africa, studies conducted in Ethiopia found that land certification programs in 1998–99 and 2003–05 resulted in more active rental markets (Holden, Deininger, and Ghebru 2009; Deininger, Ali, and Alemu 2011b).

The second factor is avoiding or eliminating controls and restrictions on land rental markets. Experience in Ethiopia and Uganda suggests that even well-intended government controls and restrictions on land rental markets that are meant to protect poor people from exploitation can end up harming them (see box 3.3). In Ethiopia, restrictions on land rental markets in all regions except Amhara reduced the opportunity to use land more productively. In Uganda, strict controls on rent and on the eviction of tenants drove landlords out of land rental markets during the 2000s. To boost land rental markets and realize their developmental benefits, Sub-Saharan countries will have to accelerate land policy reforms that strengthen land tenure security and eliminate restrictions on land rental.

Land Reforms and Interventions Promoting Gender Equity

A growing body of literature documents persistent gender gaps in African agriculture in particular and across the developing world in general (World Bank

BOX 3.3

Government Intervention and Rental Markets in Ethiopia and Uganda

Rural land in Ethiopia is owned by the state and can be neither sold nor mortgaged. Land rental is also restricted in all regions except Amhara. Evidence from Ethiopia suggests that restrictions on land rental not only reduce the opportunity to use land more productively, but also may hinder development of the nonfarm sector, as farmers who took nonfarm jobs perceived that they faced a significantly higher risk of losing land through redistribution than those who cultivated their land (Deininger et al. 2003). Land certification in 1998–99 in the Tigray region of Ethiopia increased the level of participation in the land rental market, especially that of female-headed households (Holden, Deininger, and Ghebru 2009), as participants were sure that they could get their land back after expiry of the rental contract. A later study in the Amhara region found that land certification during 2003–05 created a supply of land for the rental market (Deininger, Ali, and Alemu 2011b). These studies support the case for lifting restrictions on land rental markets in all regions of Ethiopia.

In Uganda, the first major regulation of land rental markets was enactment of the *Busuulu* (annual dues) and *Envujjo* (levy per acre) Law of 1928, which placed an upper limit on rent paid by tenants to landowners and protected tenants from being evicted without receiving compensation for land or land improvements, mainly in the Buganda and Bunyoro regions. The legislation, undertaken in response to political pressure exerted by tenants, recognized that the colonial government had unfairly given away land to Buganda chiefs and other notables under *mailo* land title (a form of freehold), without compensating customary owners (Tatwangire and Holden 2011). The 1969 Public Land Act provided customary tenants with even more protection against eviction. The 1975 Land Reform Decree nationalized all land and converted customary tenancy on *mailo* land to customary tenancy on public (state) land, but it was never enforced. In fact, while the decree was in place, land rental markets expanded rapidly, especially during the 1990s; the share of households renting land increased from 13 percent in 1992 to 36 percent in 1999 (Deininger and Mpuga 2003). However, the 1998 Land Act brought the second major regulation to land markets, and land rental markets plunged; the share of households renting fell to 17 percent in 2007 (Baland et al. 2007). The new law empowered customary tenants (so-called bona fide and lawful occupants) by fixing rent at a nominal value equivalent to US$0.60 (regardless of size, location, or quality of land) and by making it possible to register (with consent of the landlord), inherit, sell, and mortgage tenancy rights. The result was that landlords evicted tenants and disengaged from the rental market. To stem the evictions, the Land Act was amended in 2010 to make it very difficult for landlords to evict tenants, requiring a court order and making eviction a punishable offense (with jail terms up to seven years). These legal instruments had the unintended effect of discouraging landlords from renting land, ultimately hurting tenants rather than protecting them (World Bank 2012).

2011b; Bezabih and Holden 2010; Peterman, Behrman, and Quisumbing 2010). Female farmers in many parts of the developing world face many challenges in accessing productive resources such as credit, fertilizer, and land. A comprehensive analysis of case studies from five South Asian countries found that fewer women than men have command over the use of arable land, women have more limited land use rights, and many women have no control at all over production and management decisions (Agarwal 1994). The challenges facing women farmers in Africa are equally daunting. Women's rights to land and property are very limited and often depend on their marital status. Improving access to productive resources such as fertilizer and land can improve women's agricultural yields by 10 to 30 percent. At the moment, African women farmers are less productive than their male counterparts; in Ethiopia, female farmers produce 26 percent less than male farmers, while in Ghana, they produce 17 percent less (FAO 2011; World Bank 2011b). Given that more than 70 percent of farming activities in Africa are undertaken by women, improving the access of women to productive resources will invariably raise agricultural productivity and improve food security in many parts of Africa. With the increasing recognition of gender issues in land interventions, several guides have been developed, including a comprehensive training package for professionals on designing and evaluating land tools with a gender perspective (UN-Habitat, GLTN 2011).

Legal recognition of women's land rights is the first step toward reversing the discrimination against women, and the constitutions and recent land-related laws of many African countries recognize the equality of land rights (Deininger 2003). Implementation has been the primary challenge, given the discrimination ingrained in customary law. Ethiopia and Rwanda have risen to the challenge by implementing land registration programs that have successfully strengthened women's land rights (see box 3.4). Impact evaluation studies of Ethiopia's registration program found that the program improved the security of land tenure for both men and women farmers and had a positive impact on productivity, although the magnitude of the gain was greater for men than for women, suggesting that women require better access to production inputs if they are to make greater gains in productivity. An impact study of the short-term impacts of Rwanda's registration program also found that the program increased land tenure security for women by improving access to land among legally married women and by prompting better gender-neutral recording of inheritance rights; the study also found that the program led to increased investment in and maintenance of soil conservation measures, particularly among female-headed households.

Key interventions in Ethiopia and Rwanda included elevating women's secondary land rights to equal those of men, legally recognizing women's inheritance rights, and allowing the joint registration of spousal rights to land. Supporting elements in such programs included education, awareness, and

BOX 3.4

Successful Land Reforms and Women's Land Rights in Ethiopia and Rwanda

In Ethiopia, the 1975 Land Proclamation nationalized all rural land, giving all farmers a usufruct right to use the land (Bezabih and Holden 2010). And since the 1997 Federal Proclamation (law), which devolved the responsibility for land policy to the regions, and subsequent land proclamations of the main regions, both men and women are entitled to the same rights to land. However, in practice, women's rights to land depend on marriage, as their rights are registered jointly with their spouses, not separately. This has limited the access of women to land, especially widows and unmarried women. But Ethiopia's Land Certification Program, implemented in its four main regions in the late 1990s through the mid-2000s, undertook a serious effort to strengthen women's right to access land. The program issued land use certificates to both spouses, conferring equity and joint ownership. Several studies have analyzed the impact of the program on the tenure security and agricultural productivity of women farmers and found that women received land certificates either jointly or singly, with certificates that carried the names and photos of both husband and wife (Deininger, Ali, and Alemu 2011a; Bezabih and Holden 2010). The studies found that the certification program made land tenure more secure for both men and women farmers, but the productivity gains were mixed. While the program had an overall positive impact on productivity, the gains of men farmers were far greater than those of women farmers. This supports the widely held hypothesis that women farmers need better access to productive inputs, such as improved seed and fertilizer, if they are to maximize their gains from improved tenure security (Quisumbing and Pandolfelli 2008).

After emerging from genocide in 1994, Rwanda undertook considerable legal and institutional reforms in the land sector, followed by implementation of a nationwide land registration program. The 2004 national land policy and the Organic Land Law of 2005 conferred the following: (a) equal rights to daughters and sons to inherit property belonging to their parents, (b) protection of women's property rights under legally registered marriages subject to the provisions of family law, and (c) requirements for both women and men to provide consent in the case of sale, mortgage, or exchange of matrimonial property by any of the partners (Government of Rwanda 2005). With financial and technical support primarily from the U.K. Department for International Development, the government implemented a nationwide program that aims to clarify existing land rights on all of the country's estimated 10 million–11 million parcels of land (Sagashya and English 2010). A recent impact study analyzed the short-term impact of the registration program and found that it (a) improved access to land among legally married women, (b) prompted better gender-neutral recording of inheritance rights, and (c) led to increased investment and maintenance of soil conservation measures, particularly among female-headed households (Ali, Deininger, and Goldstein 2011).

information campaigns highlighting women's land rights, adequate representation of women on program implementation teams, and open and accessible appeal systems to address the concerns of aggrieved parties. The design, implementation, and results of the Ethiopian and Rwandan land registration programs imply that, when properly scaled up, these programs can reduce gender gaps, thereby addressing cultural biases and historical shortcomings of land policies in many parts of Sub-Saharan Africa.

Notes

1. While Brazil's and Malawi's approaches to land reform are similar, they are different in several respects. Brazil's program was larger (80,000 households and 1 million hectares from mid-1990s to 2008), was preceded by the introduction of a land tax and the reduction of incentives for large holdings, used loans for land acquisition and on-farm development and grants for infrastructure, and was anchored in specialized institutions and land reform legislation. Details can be found in World Bank reports (World Bank 1997, 2009).
2. The goal was to relocate 15,000 households to 33,000 hectares within five years.
3. Beneficiaries acquired mostly abandoned estates that had remained fallow for many years. Obviously, long-term impacts will depend on the capacity of farmers to manage optimal levels of inputs.
4. Report by the director general of the Department of Land Affairs to the Parliamentary Portfolio Committee on Agriculture and Land Affairs, quoted in *Farmers Weekly*, November 4, 2005.

References

Agarwal, B. 1994. *A Field of One's Own: Gender and Land Rights in South Asia*. South Asian Studies. New York: Cambridge University Press.

Ali, D. A., K. Deininger, S. Dercon, M. Hunter, J. Sanderfur, and A. Zeitlin. 2012. "Are Poor Slum-Dwellers Willing to Pay for Formal Land Title? Evidence from Dar es Salaam." Working Paper, World Bank, Washington, DC.

Ali, D., K. Deininger, and M. Goldstein. 2011. "Environmental and Gender Impacts of Land Tenure Regularization in Africa: Pilot Evidence from Rwanda." Policy Research Working Paper 5765, World Bank, Washington, DC.

Amanor, K. S., and M. K. Diderutuah. 2001. "Share Contracts in the Oil Palm and Citrus Belt of Ghana." International Institute for Environment and Development, London.

Attorney General of Kenya. 2010. "The Proposed Constitution of Kenya, 6th of May 2010." Published by the Attorney General in Accordance with Section 34 of the Constitution of Kenya Review Act, 2008 (no. 9 of 2008).

Baland, J. M., F. Gaspart, J. M. Platteau, and F. Place. 2007. "The Distributive Impact of Land Markets in Uganda." *Economic Development and Cultural Change* 55 (2): 283–311.

Bezabih, M., and S. Holden. 2010. "The Role of Land Certification in Reducing Gender Gaps in Productivity in Rural Ethiopia." EFD Discussion Paper 10–23, Environment for Development, Washington, DC, November.

Binswanger-Mkhize, H. P., C. Bourguignon, and R. van den Brink, eds. 2009. *Agricultural Land Redistribution: Toward Greater Consensus*. Washington, DC: World Bank.

Deininger, K. 2003. *Land Policies for Growth and Poverty Reduction*. World Bank Policy Research Report. Washington, DC: World Bank; New York: Oxford University Press.

Deininger, K., D. A. Ali, and T. Alemu. 2011a. "Impacts of Land Certification on Tenure Security, Investment, and Land Market Participation: Evidence from Ethiopia." *Land Economics* 87 (2): 312–34.

———. 2011b. "Productivity Effects of Land Rental Markets in Ethiopia: Evidence from a Matched Tenant-Landlord Sample." Policy Research Working Paper 5727, World Bank, Washington, DC.

Deininger, K., and G. Feder. 2009. "Land Registration, Governance, and Development: Evidence and Implications for Policy." *World Bank Research Observer* 24 (2): 233–66.

Deininger, K., and S. Jin. 2003. "Land Sales and Rental Markets in Transition: Evidence from Rural Viet Nam." Discussion Paper, World Bank, Washington, DC.

———. 2007. "Land Rental Markets in the Process of Rural Structural Transformation: Productivity and Equity Impacts in China." Policy Research Working Paper 4454, World Bank, Washington, DC.

———. 2009. "Securing Property Rights in Transition: Lessons from Implementation of China's Rural Land Contracting Law." *Journal of Economic Behavior and Organization* 70 (1–2): 22–38.

Deininger, K., S. Jin, B. Adenew, S. Gebre-Selassie, and M. Demke. 2003. "Market and Non-Market Transfers of Land in Ethiopia: Implications for Efficiency, Equity, and Nonfarm Development." Policy Research Working Paper 2992, World Bank, Washington, DC.

Deininger, K., and P. Mpuga. 2003. "Land Markets in Uganda: Incidence, Impact, and Evolution over Time." Discussion Paper, World Bank, Washington, DC.

Estudillo, J. P., A. R. Quisumbing, and K. Otsuka. 2001. "Gender Differences in Land Inheritance and Schooling Investments in the Rural Philippines." *London Economics* 77 (1): 130–43.

FAO (Food and Agriculture Organization of the United Nations). 2011. *The State of Food and Agriculture 2010–2011*. Rome: FAO.

Field, E. 2005. "Property Rights and Investment in Urban Slums." *Journal of the European Economic Association* 3 (2–3): 279–90.

Friedman, J., E. Jimenez, and S. K. Mayo. 1988. "The Demand for Tenure Security in Developing Countries." *Journal of Development Economics* 29 (2): 185–98.

Galiani, S., and E. Schargrodsky. 2005. "Property Rights for the Poor: Effects of Land Titling." Documento de Trabajo 06/2005, Universidad Torcuato Di Tella, Centro de Investigacion en Finanzas, Buenos Aires.

Government of Rwanda. 2005. "Organic Law No. 08/2005 of 14/07/2005: Determining the Use and Management of Land in Rwanda." Government of Rwanda, Kigali.

Government of South Africa. 1997. "White Paper on South African Land Policy." Department of Land Affairs, Pretoria.

———. 2011. "Government's Proposed Solution to the Land Question." Green Paper on land reform, Department of Rural Development and Land Reform, Pretoria. Adopted by the cabinet on August 24. http://www.politicsweb.co.za/politicsweb/view/politicsweb/en/page71656?oid=253690&sn=Detail&pid=71616.

Gulyani, S., D. Talukdar, and D. Jack. 2010. "Poverty, Living Conditions, and Infrastructure Access: A Comparison of Nairobi, Dakar, and Johannesburg." Policy Research Working Paper 5388, World Bank, Washington, DC.

Hall, Ruth. 2003. *Farm Tenure.* Evaluating Land and Agrarian Reform in South Africa Series 3. Cape Town: University of the Western Cape, Programme for Land and Agrarian Studies.

Holden, S. T., K. Deininger, and H. Ghebru. 2009. "Impacts of Low-Cost Land Certification on Investment and Productivity." *American Journal of Agricultural Economics* 91 (2): 359–73.

Johnson, D. G. 2000. "Can Agricultural Labor Adjustment Occur Primarily through Creation of Rural Non-Farm Jobs in China?" *Urban Studies* 39 (12): 2163–74.

Kevane, M. 1996. "Agrarian Structure and Agricultural Practice: Typology and Application to Western Sudan." *American Journal of Agricultural Economics* 78 (1): 236–45.

Lahiff, E., and G. Li. 2012. "Land Redistribution in South Africa: A Critical Review." Working Paper for the "Land Administration and Reform in SSA" study, World Bank, Washington, DC.

Lloyd, I. 2012. "Experiences with Regularization of Land Tenure in Urban Informal Settlements in Kenya, Tanzania, and Lesotho." Working Paper for the "Land Administration and Reform in SSA" study, World Bank, Washington, DC.

MCC (Millennium Challenge Corporation). 2011. "Lesotho Compact, Quarterly Status Report." MCC, Washington, DC, September.

Peterman, A., J. Behrman, and A. Quisumbing. 2010. "A Review of Empirical Evidence on Gender Differences in Non-land Agricultural Inputs, Technology, and Services in Developing Countries." Poverty, Health, and Nutrition Division, International Food Policy Research Institute, Washington, DC.

Place, F. 2002. "Land Markets in Africa: Preconditions, Potentials, and Limitations." Paper presented at the Regional Workshop, "Land Issues in the Africa, Middle East, and North Africa Region," Kampala, April 29–May 2.

Quisumbing, A., and L. Pandolfelli. 2008. "Promising Approaches to Address the Needs of Poor Female Farmers." IFPRI Note 13, International Food Policy Research Institute, Washington, DC.

Sagashya, D., and C. English. 2010. "Designing and Establishing a Land Administration System for Rwanda: Technical and Economic Analysis." In *Innovations in Land Rights Recognition, Administration, and Governance,* edited by K. Deininger, C. Augustinus, P. Munro-Faure, and S. Enemark. Washington, DC: World Bank.

Simtowe, F., J. Mangisoni, and M. Mendola. 2011. "Independent Project Impact Evaluation of the Malawi Community-Based Rural Land Development Project." First draft report, ITALTREND, Reggio Emilia, Italy.

Tatwangire, A., and S. T. Holden. 2011. "Welfare Effects of Market Friendly Land Reforms in Uganda." Working Paper 02/11, Center for Land Tenure Studies, Norwegian University of Life Sciences, Aas, Norway.

Tchale, H. 2012. "Pilot Redistributive Land Reform in Malawi: Innovations and Emerging Good Practices." Working Paper for the "Land Administration and Reform in SSA" study, World Bank, Washington, DC.

UNFPA (United Nations Population Fund). 2011. *The State of World Population 2011: People and Possibilities in a World of 7 Billion*. New York: UNFPA.

UN-Habitat (United Nations Habitat). 2003. *The Challenge of Slums: Global Report on Human Settlements, 2003*. London: Earthscan.

UN-Habitat (United Nations Habitat), GLTN (Global Land Tool Network). 2011. "Designing and Evaluating Land Tools with a Gender Perspective: A Training Package for Land Professionals." United Nations Habitat, GLTN, Nairobi, May 31. http://www.gltn.net/en/home/gender/designing-and-evaluating-land-tools-with-a-gender-perspective-/download.html.

United Republic of Kenya. n.d. *Kenya Slum Upgrading Programme (KENSUP), 2005–2020, Implementation Strategy*. Vol. 1. Nairobi: Government Printer.

———. 2009. "Sessional Paper No. 3 of 2009 on National Land Policy, August 2009." Government Printer for the Ministry of Lands, Nairobi.

United Republic of Tanzania. 1972. "National Sites and Services and Squatter Upgrading Programme." Government of Tanzania, Dar es Salaam.

———. 2011. "National Program for Regularization and Prevention of Unplanned Settlements, 2012–2021." Ministry of Lands, Housing, and Human Settlement Development, Dar es Salaam, February.

Van Royen, J. C. 2009. "Land Reform in South Africa: Effects on Land Prices and Productivity." Rhodes University, Grahamstown.

Velente, C. 2009. "Food (In)Security Impact of Land Redistribution in South Africa: Microeconomic Evidence from National Level Data." *World Development* 37 (9): 1540–53.

World Bank. 1997. "Brazil Land Reform and Poverty Alleviation Pilot Project." Project Appraisal Document, World Bank, Washington, DC.

———. 2004a. "Local Government Support Project." Project Appraisal Document, World Bank, Washington, DC.

———. 2004b. "Malawi Community-Based Rural Land Development Project." Project Appraisal Document, World Bank, Washington, DC.

———. 2005. "Tanzania Private Sector Competitiveness Project." Project Appraisal Document, World Bank, Washington, DC.

———. 2006. "Inside Informality: Poverty, Jobs, Housing, and Services in Nairobi's Slums." Report 36347-KE, Urban and Water Unit 1, Africa Region World Bank, Washington, DC.

———. 2008. *World Development Report 2009: Reshaping Economic Geography*. Washington, DC: World Bank.

———. 2009. "Brazil Land-Based Poverty Alleviation 1." Implementation Completion and Results Report, World Bank, Washington, DC.

————. 2011a. "Kenya Informal Settlements Improvement Project." Project Appraisal Document, World Bank, Washington, DC.

————. 2011b. *World Development Report 2012: Gender Equality and Development.* Washington, DC: World Bank.

————. 2012. "Uganda: Making Growth More Inclusive: Transforming Farms, Human Capital, and Geography." Synthesis Report, World Bank, Washington, DC.

Zhai, F., T. Hertel, and Z. Wang. 2003. "Labor Market Distortions, Rural-Urban Inequality, and the Opening of China's Economy." Working Paper 27, Global Trade Analysis Project (GTAP), Center for Global Trade Analysis, Purdue University, Lafayette, IN.

Chapter 4

Land Administration for Good Governance and Conflict Management

The role of land policies in ensuring social stability and good governance cannot be overemphasized, as broken land-related laws and conflicts have often led to a breakdown of governance, social instability, and even civil war. For example, unresolved claims for restitution of land rights in former settler colonies, especially in Kenya, South Africa, and Zimbabwe, have been a bone of contention historically and an ongoing source of social instability. Conflicts over land arising from global commercial interests in natural resources have been a common occurrence in countries such as the Democratic Republic of Congo, Liberia, and Sierra Leone. And pervasive land disputes associated with access to land for returning refugees and internally displaced people in conflict-afflicted countries such as Burundi, Côte d'Ivoire, Rwanda, Somalia, South Sudan, and Uganda have been common, at times reviving old conflicts and inciting civil wars. Good land policies, good laws and regulations, and respect for the law can go a long way toward improving governance and managing conflict. This chapter reviews five topics of considerable relevance to governance and conflict management in Sub-Saharan Africa:

- Managing conflict by building competent and impartial institutions for resolving land disputes
- Strengthening governance and property rights by improving land acquisition laws and procedures
- Strengthening management of public land and reducing corruption by creating inventories of government land
- Grappling with governance issues associated with converting rural to urban land use
- Managing conflict by developing land administration in postconflict states.

High Court in Greater Accra and expects to scale these up to other parts of the country in the near future. In principle, land courts entail an expedited process, with cases handled by judges better trained in the complexity of land law than is typical in general courts.

Early evaluations of Ghana's experience, however, suggest that land courts remain vulnerable to many of the same problems that afflict the court system overall. In fact, a report financed by the World Bank calculated that the time required to resolve cases in land courts exceeds that in ordinary courts, with only 14 percent resolved by the land court within a year of being filed (World Bank 2010). This disappointing performance was attributed to several factors. First, the creation of land courts was not accompanied by a significant reform of the rules and procedures governing land cases. Hence, unlike the new stream-lined commercial courts, in which simplified procedural rules have dramatically improved case management, cases entering land courts remain susceptible to the same complexities, delay tactics, and setbacks they would have encountered in ordinary courts. Second, as in ordinary courts, insufficient attention is paid to pretrial processing of cases. Improved performance will require placing more emphasis on seeking settlements, as an effort to seek settlement once the process has started is made in only 8 percent of cases (Kotey 2004), on screening out frivolous claims, and on preparing better evidentiary submissions in advance (requiring time-consuming inputs from surveyors or the land registry). Ghana's chief justice recently emphasized the importance of training judges and other court officers in alternative dispute resolution (ADR) techniques in hopes of diverting cases away from full-fledged treatment by land courts.

Similar lessons emerge from Tanzania, where a 2002 law established a new structure of land courts with four tiers (village councils, ward land tribunals, district land and housing tribunals, and a land division of the High Court). According to a recent World Bank study, introduction of this system has not stemmed the accumulation of unresolved cases (Deininger, Selod, and Burns 2012). Here again, evidence points to the need for undertaking procedural reforms and changes in institutional culture, rather than for creating specialized tribunals alone.

Addressing weak capacity of courts and training of judges   The phenomenon of low professional standards among judges affects African judicial systems generally. While not limited to land issues, the problem plays a significant role in the weakness of land administration across the continent. The complexity of land law has always posed a challenge for undertrained judges. In recent years, the demands on the competency of judges have increased with the passage of new land laws requiring a more careful and nuanced understanding of the relationship between statutory rules and customary norms. Yet efforts to build this understanding among judges have often lagged. A telling anecdote from Mozambique reveals that as late as 2002, five years after passage of one of when livelihoods are land based. Provisions are usually made to pay cash for nonland assets and crops, but where land rights themselves are ill-defined, are legal but lack documentation, or fall short of "ownership," those rights tend to be compensated at a very low rate. Finally, even in areas (usually urban) where ownership has been formalized and documented and land markets exist, outdated or nonindependent valuation techniques frequently result in "market values" that are significantly lower than would be required to replace the land through a real market purchase.

Expansive Scope of Takings Powers

In most countries, the government's ability to invoke powers of compulsory acquisition is limited by law or constitution to land required for a public purpose or use. Defining such terms has often been controversial. A general principle is that the takings power is an extraordinary one, intended to meet genuine public needs that cannot be met efficiently through market operations or other voluntary arrangements; it is not intended to support primarily private gain. Drawing this line has always been difficult, and the public-purpose concept has in some African countries lent itself to broad interpretations that facilitate land being taken by the government in favor of powerful private actors (World Resources Institute 2001). In recent years, this controversy has played out in the area of large-scale land acquisitions for commercial agriculture, a phenomenon touted by some as an inevitable part of unlocking the economic potential of African agriculture and criticized by others as a government-facilitated land grab by private investors (Deininger, Ali, and Alemu 2011). In several countries (Ethiopia and Tanzania, for example), government land acquisition for commercial agriculture is specifically listed as a public purpose. While a particular investment may have genuine public (local and national) benefits, they are often ephemeral, local land rights are not properly taken into account, and the invocation of the government's takings power undermines the ability of the local population to negotiate directly with investors and benefit from an investment.

Governance Shortcomings

Finally, the African experience with compulsory acquisition has (as elsewhere in the world) suffered from a variety of governance deficiencies. Numerous examples exist of long-standing complaints from displaced people concerning the underpayment or nonpayment of compensation or delays in payment that have continued for many years (see box 4.1). Similarly, sometimes land takings have not been completed, and existing rights have been officially expunged without taking further action, leaving occupants in place but in legal limbo (Keith et al. 2008).

BOX 4.1

Land Acquisition and Compensation in Ghana

Ghana is coming to grips with a difficult legacy of extensive compulsory acquisitions, while thinking creatively about legal and policy reforms to modernize its land acquisition process. Continuing a trend well under way at the end of the colonial period, Ghanaian governments pursued an aggressive campaign of land acquisition in the first three decades of independence, acquiring more than 100,000 hectares of land. The largest expanses of acquired land were intended to support agricultural schemes and forestry operations, but substantial amounts of land were also targeted for hydroelectric development, residential development, and other development uses. A comprehensive study of acquisitions over this period highlights key problems that are similar in nature, if not in detail, to those found in many other countries in Africa and elsewhere (Larbi, Antwi, and Olomolaiye 2004):

- *Nonpayment or underpayment of compensation.* Compensation has not yet been paid for nearly 80 percent of all land acquired in Ghana since independence, and hundreds of cases have been lodged in court as a result. This has been facilitated by legal provisions that vest land in the government immediately upon issuance of an executive instrument, making payment of required compensation a postacquisition obligation that in many cases has not been fulfilled.

- *Poor management of and planning for acquired land.* Information about acquired land is often missing or inaccurate, contributing to confusion about the extent and location of state land. Acquired land has been particularly susceptible to encroachment or continued occupation by existing residents due to government delays in taking possession of the land and putting it to use. Acquisitions are rarely accompanied by any strategic planning or budgeting for eventual use of the land, contributing to nonuse or misuse once land has been transferred to the state.

- *Change of use.* Some land has been diverted from its intended public use to private development, facilitated by the pre-1992 constitution standard that the Ghanaian government could acquire land "for any purpose which in the opinion of the Government would be for the benefit of the country as a whole."

The 1992 constitution articulated the need to reform compulsory acquisition practices, including tighter provisions concerning public purposes for land, clearer justification for its acquisition, and a preemption right for former owners in the event that land is not used for its intended public purpose. The 1999 national land policy clearly indicated that prior acquisitions and current practices were in urgent need of attention, and successive governments have moved to address these issues. As described elsewhere in this chapter, a state land inventory was piloted to help the government to identify and document prior acquisitions better. This is expected to inform a process of selective return of unused land in some cases and to aid negotiation of the amount of

(continued next page)

Box 4.1 (continued)

outstanding compensation in others. Ongoing drafting of a new Lands Bill is expected to address compulsory acquisition in detail, updating obsolete provisions in existing statutes and reforming features that have led to abuse in the past (such as the absence of requirements that compensation be paid prior to acquisition and that acquisition be preceded by diligent public notification and consultation). Notably, under the Ghana commercial agricultural project, the government recently took the position that the use of compulsory acquisition in support of private large-scale investments in agricultural land should be discouraged in favor of voluntary and transparent negotiations between investors and communities (World Bank 2012).

Lessons from Experience for Strengthening Governance and Property Rights

While land acquisition and compensation are embodied in complex governance issues with equally complex solutions, a few lessons can guide some African countries that are embarking on a path of reform in this area:

- Updating laws to keep pace with innovations in land policy, especially recognition of multiple land tenure systems, including customary tenure
- Avoiding the undervaluing of land rights and poorly tailored forms of compensation
- Avoiding extending the principle of government takings of land in the "public interest" to include acquisition of land for investment
- Addressing deficiencies in governance such as underpayment and no payment of compensation or prolonged delays in compensation.

Strengthening Management of Public Land and Reducing Corruption by Creating Inventories of Government Land

State landownership is widespread in Sub-Saharan Africa. Many countries inherited legal provisions at independence that promoted the concept of public land, including unused customary land, which governments readily used or simply claimed. Countries with colonial white settlements (such as Angola, Botswana, Kenya, Malawi, Mozambique, Namibia, Swaziland, Zambia, and Zimbabwe) nationalized settlers' farmlands or corporate farms after independence. During the 1970s, countries such as Benin, Burkina Faso, Nigeria, and Uganda either nationalized private and customary lands or established a state monopoly over land allocation, using this as a carte blanche to expand government landownership; this often created conditions for high levels of mismanagement and corruption (Mabogunje 1992). Ghana's experience illustrates the extent of state landownership: as of 2000, the state owned about 40 percent of all urban and periurban lands, most of which were undeveloped (Kasanga and Kotey 2001). Leaving land unused or poorly used has a high opportunity cost, since the land could be put to better use.

While auctioning state land for private sector development is one option, there are other efficient and equitable uses of state lands. For example, where private citizens have occupied or used state land informally for a long time, such as in rural and urban informal settlements or on agricultural land, long-term occupants could be legally recognized as owners and given land rights documents, as Kenya's new land policy has done (United Republic of Kenya 2010; World Bank 2011b). Unoccupied or underused state land could also be sold to land-poor farmers, as was done under a community-based land reform program in Malawi (World Bank 2004; Tchale 2012).

To undertake any of these options, however, governments must first be able to identify and establish the ownership and occupancy status of government-owned lands. Currently, many African governments do not know the extent of their state landownership, as most lands are not surveyed and registered; in addition, they do not have up-to-date information on the current status of ownership and occupancy. To overcome this information gap and generate information for policy and decision making, some governments have started inventorying government-owned land. Successful completion should lay the foundation for improved management of state lands in Sub-Sahran Africa.

To date, Ghana's systematic and substantial inventory of its state lands has been the most successful, while Uganda's inventory is more recent and more limited in scale (see box 4.2). Ghana initiated its land inventory exercises in 2003 with two objectives: (a) to enable land sector agencies to obtain up-to-date, accurate records on all government-acquired and -occupied lands and (b) to enable the government to formulate and implement policy guidelines on compulsory acquisition, compensation, and divestiture of public lands no longer needed for their intended public purpose (World Bank 2003; Ahene 2012). Inventory exercises were undertaken by 10 consulting firms, covering 722 out of an estimated 1,144 sites (63 percent). The exercises provided a clearer picture of the composition of government land and the principal sources of tension in communities affected by government land acquisitions. They also helped the government to issue short-term policy guidelines for managing state land assets, while waiting for results of the completed national inventory. Uganda's land inventory exercise was conducted from 2009 to 2011 and covered only 10 percent of the country's state lands. It faced design and implementation

BOX 4.2

Challenges and Opportunities for State Land Inventories to Improve Land Management in Ghana and Uganda

Ghana has a large stock of government land, accumulated mainly during the 1950s under the radical land policies of Kwame Nkrumah. In 2001, the Ghanaian government owned an estimated 40 percent of urban and periurban land (Kasanga and Kotey 2001). To improve the management of state land, from 2003 to 2010, the government of Ghana worked to establish a national inventory of acquired, occupied, and vested state lands, with the objective of acquiring accurate information for use in public land management decisions. Information on location, size, ownership, and boundary measurements of land, as well as on current land use and encumbrances, including squatters, was desired. In all, 10 consulting firms undertook 10 pilot inventory exercises in 3 regions of the country: 1,144 sites were identified, significantly greater than the 288 sites compiled from the records of public sector land agencies. The exercise provided a clearer picture of the composition of government land and the principal sources of tension in communities affected by government land acquisitions. For example, of the 722 sites inventoried, only 58 (less than 10 percent) were formally acquired, compensated for, and fully used for their intended purpose; 198 sites (27 percent) were occupied and used by state agencies without any formal acquisition; the acquisition status of 377 sites could not be established (52 percent); and 6 sites reserved by the state were never formally acquired and were not being used for the intended purpose. The exercise led to capacity building in both the public and private sectors for future inventory operations and enabled the government to issue short-term policy guidelines for managing state land assets. A comprehensive policy will be prepared after additional inventory exercises cover the remaining sites in the country.

Uganda's large stock of government land was accumulated gradually through a process of expropriation that started with the 1900 Buganda land agreement (West 1964) and continued after independence, permitted through various constitutional and legal instruments. To improve efficiency and transparency of government land management, the government of Uganda undertook an exercise from July 2009 to December 2011 to establish a national inventory of government lands under a World Bank–funded project (World Bank 2005). Its objective was similar to that of Ghana: to provide an accurate record of government land to give policy makers reliable information with which to make public land management decisions.

Uganda's state land inventory exercise was poorly executed, however, and even though it employed a methodology similar to that used in Ghana, the Uganda pilot was less successful in all regards. A single private contractor was hired to ascertain the stock of approximately 12,000 government land parcels in 80 districts. By the end of the 30-month contract period, only 1,200 sites (10 percent) in 4 districts had been surveyed. The contracted firm was less successful in sensitizing the community and

(continued next page)

Box 4.2 (continued)

suffered various setbacks in the field. First, it could not survey lands donated to the government by religious and traditional authorities because these donors contested the donations and there were no clear policy guidelines to adjudicate such claims. Second, staff limitations at the district and central government levels were a serious bottleneck to efficient checking of cadastral data, which significantly delayed the government's approval of the survey results. Third, the exercise was opposed by some communities and thus received limited cooperation from area land committees and district land boards. As a result, approval and analysis of the surveyed work was only possible following technical and financial interventions, and the low proportion of state lands inventoried (10 percent) was insufficient for policy making. The inventory will be continued under a follow-up World Bank project, now in the early stages of planning and preparation.

Source: Adapted from Ahene 2012.

---

problems that will be corrected before a follow-up project resumes the effort (Ahene 2012). The Ghanaian and Ugandan land inventories generated several lessons and best practices that can inform other African countries contemplating similar activities (Ahene 2012):

- Land inventory activities should be undertaken by specialized interdisciplinary teams of professionals drawn from the public and private sectors, with clearly defined responsibilities. Ghana's land inventory was executed by four teams of field officers, of which two were survey teams and two were valuation and land use planning teams.

- Sensitization and training activities should be conducted by a carefully appointed interdisciplinary team of public and private sector professionals.

- A list of government-acquired and -occupied lands compiled from various sources should be verified publicly before the list is finalized and used as a basis to contract out land inventories.

- Additional human and financial resources for processing and handling data should be acquired to avoid disrupting normal land services, given the volume of data produced by a comprehensive land inventory.

- In most typical settings, the private sector should undertake the field boundary survey, collect survey data, and prepare deed and survey plans, while the public sector should undertake quality assurance, approval of survey and deed plans, and title registration.

Grappling with Governance Issues Associated with Converting Rural to Urban Land Use

Normally, land prices are driven by the decisions of individual players in land markets.[1] Occasionally, however, they are also driven by changes in land use regulations, as happens in rural-urban land conversions. Regulation of land use, such as zoning, is justified by the need to protect the public interest against irrational land use by individuals. In countries with good governance, when a change in zoning results in an increase in land values, the increase is normally subject to a tax used to benefit a larger segment of the public. However, in countries with inadequate land laws or poor enforcement of them, increases in land values resulting from rezoning are often not taxed at all or are undertaxed. The benefits are captured by speculators and rent seekers, including those who have access to insider information about the planned changes in zoning. This section reviews governance challenges involving rural-urban and public-private conversion of land, using Nairobi, Kenya, as an example.

A recent study of periurban land use conversion in Nairobi found that informal networks of politicians, bureaucrats (especially in the Commissioner of Lands Office), professionals, and citizens operate in a system characterized by (a) strong institutional incentives to work around expensive, cumbersome, and highly bureaucratic formal land management processes that have convenient loopholes; (b) brokers who gain private benefits by using privileged access to flawed land management institutions, information, and mechanisms to formalize land rights through some form of government-issued document; and (c) financial incentives to avoid any kind of planning that may lead private developers, local officials, and environmental consultants or auditors to collude in circumventing controls (Ngau et al. 2010).

Further, the study found that both contests and collusive games within and across professional associations and the ruling class led to enactment of the Physical Planning Act, while preserving the original law. This contributed to the current formal system of laws governing rural to urban land conversion in Kenya, which are complex and in conflict with overlapping subject matter jurisdictions. Specifically, land management laws have provisions for three parallel formal development pathways, the preferred path being the one with the least public scrutiny, even though it is the most expensive. This situation has negatively affected Nairobi's growth. The city is characterized by a lack of services or ad hoc self-help provision of services, rural-urban conflicts over land use, environmental degradation, and a host of other complex problems (Memon 1982; Thuo 2010). These dynamics have special implications for the poor who, despite the availability of urban land for housing even in Nairobi's core, do not have adequate access to land through formal delivery systems; they only have it through informal delivery systems that require connections (Musyoka 2004; Huchzermeyer 2008). In addition, influential persons sometimes use the poor to assist in irregular appropriation of land, the predominant means of accessing land. In such cases, the poor are often further displaced through the high cost of formalizing the land or insecure tenure (see box 4.3).

BOX 4.3

The "Ngwata" System of Land Conversion in Mlolongo Town of Mayoko Municipal Council

In Mlolongo, Kenya, land was forcefully seized by councilors in 2000 and allocated to individuals connected to them, following the role of patronage. Called *ngwata*, this type of land allocation process is similar to grabbing, implying the irregular or illegitimate acquisition of land (United Republic of Kenya 2001, 2004; Klopp 2000; Olima 1997). The Municipal Council of Mavoko, in which Mlolongo falls, issued temporary occupation licenses to plot beneficiaries and encouraged them to form an association. The council then stopped dealing directly with developers, leaving this to the landowners association. A study revealed that the landowners association formed a parallel land registry office, run by officials of the Mavoko Land Association (ngwata group), in connivance with Municipal Council officials. The land registry is responsible for approving land transfers, for handling registration and related transactions, and even for issuing its own version of land titles to landowners. Field interviews revealed that council officials, politicians, and central government officials used the amorphous landowners association as a cover to acquire private and public land. While this land "invasion" was made to look like an action of the land-hungry poor, the study found that the council and politicians used it as a tactic to invade private and public land while evading court litigation from landowners and backlash from developers.

After the land appropriation in Mlolongo, untrained local people and area councilors used ropes to subdivide the land into plots for sale. These plots were eventually shared among the councilors, their political supporters, and council employees who colluded with the councilors and were paid in land for their cooperation. Some of those who benefited from the land allocation in Mlolongo, however, opted to sell their land to developers. Later, the Municipal Council of Mavoko tried to formalize the otherwise informal allocation of land in Mlolongo by issuing temporary occupancy licenses to these developers and other land beneficiaries. Once formalization started, the poorer beneficiaries of the land were unable to pay the land rates and other expenses linked to formalization and were forced to sell, illustrating that land invasions seemingly undertaken by the poor often help middle- and higher-income residents to acquire land.

Source: Adapted from Ngau et al. 2010.

Nairobi's rapid physical and population growth has occurred in the context of a series of ineffective attempts at planning. The 1963 boundary remains the official boundary to date (an area of 684 square kilometers). In 2009, the Ministry of Nairobi Metropolitan Development was established to "manage the Nairobi Metropolis by providing sustainable infrastructural services and high-quality life to all its residents, visitors, and investors." The ministry proposed extending the metropolitan region to 3,000 square kilometers and developed a "Vision Metro 2030" to turn Nairobi into a "world-class metropolis" (United Republic of Kenya 2008). This vision statement triggered land speculation in the metropolitan region and is still highly contentious (Omwenga 2008). Nairobi's growth is linked to that of several centers in periurban areas of the city that have experienced rapid population growth as a result of their advantageous location. Under the new constitution, the current "Nairobi City" will become one of 47 county governments, surrounded by the counties of Kajiado, Kiambu, and Machakos. Managing land use within this galaxy of metropolitan municipalities, including urban-rural fringes that transverse county boundaries, will require reimagining, reengineering, and reconfiguring not only land use and metropolitan planning but also a clear institutional framework.

With the advent of Kenya's new national land policy (United Republic of Kenya 2009) and constitutional reform process, the legal, institutional, and policy frameworks associated with land are currently under review. The new constitution clearly specifies that Nairobi will be restructured as a county that is also a city. National legislation for the governance and management of urban areas and counties stipulated in the new constitution has yet to be written, so the full impacts of these changes are unpredictable. However, careful research and analysis should inform the process of defining Nairobi's metropolitan area and management and should extend to Kenya's expanding periurban or rural-urban fringes.

The case of rural-urban conversion in Kenya provides one key lesson: adequate laws and effective enforcement mechanisms have to be put in place to mitigate possible collusion among networks of politicians, public officials responsible for enforcing the law, real estate brokers, and private developers who break the law to benefit from rezoning at the expense of society.

Managing Conflict by Developing Land Administration in Postconflict States

Postconflict countries often experience continuing tensions over land that are grounded in issues that predate the original conflict and may even have contributed to it. Actions taken during the period of conflict can also exacerbate land problems. For example, even though Burundi's conflicts have declined considerably, tensions over land persist, as returning refugees are resettled and others wait for resettlement. Dealing decisively with land issues at the cessation of conflict is critical not only to break the vicious cycle of conflict but also to support postconflict economic recovery. Some countries have done this successfully. For example, Cambodia avoided a recurrence of conflict by basing land rights on occupancy, resettling displaced people, and permitting the military to use lands occupied in the war zone until they were demobilized and reintegrated; this contributed to postwar reconstruction as well as to peace (Zimmermann 2002; Torhonen and Palmer 2004). Similarly, Mozambique resettled 5 million people after its peace agreement, using local institutions to mediate and resolve emerging conflicts, while also working on a new land law to provide a right of occupancy to rural families; these efforts contributed to the country's social and economic stability (Tanner 2002).

A review of Liberia's and Rwanda's experiences with reestablishing systems of land administration and embarking on needed reforms provides lessons and best practices for African countries in postconflict situations (see box 4.4; Bruce 2012). In both countries, land issues quickly came to the forefront of

BOX 4.4

Managing Conflict through Land Administration in Liberia and Rwanda

When liberated slaves and black freemen (called Americo-Liberians) returned from America beginning in the 1820s, they were granted and later sold freeholds to land that belonged to indigenous Liberians, originally in townships and then in coastal areas and hinterlands. The system was solidly grounded in Liberia's constitution, statute, and common law, and a deed registry system started in the 1850s provided validation and public recording of the new deeds. This land appropriation for Americo-Liberians, which dispossessed indigenous populations and bred resentment, contributed directly to the 1980 military overthrow of the elected government and started Liberia down the path to civil war. To be successful, any solution will have to resolve these historically rooted land grievances.

At the end of the civil war in 1997, Liberia faced many land management challenges. Its capacity to handle land policy and administration was badly degraded; authority over government land was fragmented across weak agencies lacking staff and equipment, and the records of its deeds registry had been compromised by fraud and were incomplete and physically damaged. In addition to resettling displaced people, the government focused attention on ad hoc land commissions and ADR approaches in counties with endemic land disputes. In 2009, Liberia's Governance Commission created a Land Commission to propose policy and legal reforms and to coordinate all government activities in the land sector. The president appointed a new commission

(continued next page)

Box 4.4 (continued)

in 2010, with a five-year lifetime, extendable if needed for two additional years. Substantial donor resources support the commission and other land sector agencies, not only in undertaking policy and legal work, but also in rehabilitating the technical land agencies and their activities.

At the end of the civil war and genocide in 1994, Rwanda's chronic land problem was one of the most challenging issues in postconflict reconstruction. Radical displacement of populations and the return of refugees from different ethnic groups created special difficulties for the restitution of land, while extremely high population pressure (population density averaged 479 per square kilometer) meant that no surplus land was available. Land administration was further complicated by previous appropriations of land from those who had fled and readjustments among those who had conflicting claims. In the early stages of refugee return, the government resettled many returnees in villages rather than on their homesteads, creating a new set of issues, as the rights to the land were often not clear and cultivable land was often not available nearby. Furthermore, landownership is skewed in Rwanda: 24 percent of households control roughly 70 percent of arable land, while more than one-third of rural households hold only about one-tenth of a hectare. To cap it all, Rwanda has a long history of intense competition over land and grievances over land dispossessions, often framed in terms of ethnic conflict between Hutu and Tutsi. Given these circumstances, tenure security was an urgent concern of the postwar government.

In 1997, the government began work to legislate a Torrens-style registration system (under which less than 10 percent of the land had been registered). According to the new law, enacted in July 2005, all land belongs to the Rwandan people, is managed by the state, and is made available to private users under leases of between 3 and 99 years by newly created local land commissions. Leaseholds may be transferred or mortgaged with the consent of spouses and children. Customary holdings are converted to leaseholds, and customary tenure and its institutions are abolished. Registration of land rights is mandatory, and systematic registration is authorized. A 2006 pilot informed a 2009 nationwide program to register lands using maps produced from aerial photographs. As of 2010, the program had demarcated more than 2.2 million plots and was producing about 250,000 plots per month. It is expected to register all land (estimated at 8 million parcels) by the end of 2013, at a cost per parcel of US$7–US$10. A World Bank evaluation found that only 2.5 years after completion of the pilot, a large majority of those involved viewed the process as fair and transparent; the program also increased investment and improved access to land for legally married women (Ali, Deininger, and Goldstein 2011). While the national land registration program has been successful, its sustainability depends on development of adequate institutions and incentives to register inheritances and transactions. In addition, it will be necessary to minimize and mitigate any disputes arising from the ongoing land consolidation program (and any residual land sharing) and possible claims that may arise from returnees still outside the country.

Source: Adapted from Bruce 2012.

---

postconflict national concerns, and both governments appreciated the serious-ness of the issues. In addition, development partners made funding available to address them, if somewhat belatedly. At the same time, the ability to cope with policy and management issues was badly degraded by the conflict in both coun-tries, and many years passed before either government could seriously engage in these issues.

In Rwanda, extremely high population pressure on land contributed to the initial conflict and complicates current attempts to appropriate the land of those who fled and to make readjustments for sharing land and resettling returned refugees. In Liberia, prewar tensions created by Americo-Liberians' land appropriations persist and are exacerbated by the major population dis-placement that occurred during the conflict. The two countries took different tracks in developing and implementing land policy reform strategies: Rwanda moved more quickly on systematic registration of land rights, while Liberia, arguably taking a more considered approach, focused on policy, law reform, and rebuilding government capacity. Their experiences suggest that postconflict governments and donors need to focus early not only on managing conflicts but also on developing basic land policies to address underlying tensions over land and on rebuilding land administration and management capabilities. The donor community should provide early support for these activities, which may require expanding the parameters for the use of peace-building funds in the early postconflict years.

Land dispute resolution activities can buy time in the immediate postcon-flict period, but usually do not address underlying sources of tension or pre-vent future conflicts over land. Moving more rapidly into policy work requires earlier deployment of development agencies' expertise on land tenure to assist governments struggling with land policy issues. Rebuilding the capacity of gov-ernments to administer and manage land and to resolve land disputes requires reestablishing technical capacity and retraining staff in the basics of manage-ment. Where land governance institutions are very weak or simply not present, governments will initially need to resort to institutional approaches, such as task forces and special commissions that can bring together existing expertise to focus on land matters. Given that postconflict situations differ substantially, the balance struck among conflict management, policy work, and rebuilding of capacities and institutions will necessarily vary from case to case.

Postconflict land administration in Liberia and Rwanda offers the following lessons:

- Postconflict governments and donors need to focus early not only on man-aging conflicts but also on (a) developing basic land policies to address underlying tensions over land and (b) rebuilding land administration and management capabilities.

- Land dispute resolution activities can buy time in the immediate postconflict period, but they usually do not address underlying sources of tension or prevent future conflicts over land.

- Moving more rapidly into policy work requires earlier deployment of development agencies' expertise on land tenure to assist governments struggling with land policy issues.

- Rebuilding the capacity of governments to administer and manage land and to resolve land disputes requires reestablishing technical capacity and retraining staff in the basics of management.

- Where land governance institutions are very weak or simply not present, governments will initially need to resort to institutional approaches such as task forces and special commissions that can bring together existing expertise to focus on land matters.

Note

1. This section draws generously from Ngau et al. (2010), especially from their research findings on rural-urban land conversions in Kenya. Their contribution is much appreciated.

References

Ahene, R. 2012. "A Review of Government Land Inventories in Ghana and Uganda." Working Paper for the "Land Administration and Reform in SSA" study, World Bank, Washington, DC.

Ali, D., K. Deininger, and M. Goldstein. 2011. "Environmental and Gender Impacts of Land Tenure Regularization in Africa: Pilot Evidence from Rwanda." Policy Research Working Paper 5765, World Bank, Washington, DC.

Bruce, J. 2012. "Land Administration Challenges in Post-Conflict States in Sub-Saharan Africa: Lessons from Rwanda and Liberia." Working Paper for the "Land Administration and Reforms in SSA" study, World Bank, Washington, DC.

Commission on Legal Empowerment of the Poor. 2008. *Making the Law Work for Everyone*. Vol. II. New York: United Nations Development Programme.

Crook, R. 2011. "The State and Accessible Justice in Africa: Is Ghana Unique?" Policy Brief 3, Overseas Development Institute, Africa Power and Politics, London, November.

Deininger, K., D. A. Ali, and T. Alemu. 2011. "Productivity Effects of Land Rental Markets in Ethiopia: Evidence from a Matched Tenant-Landlord Sample." Policy Research Working Paper 5727, World Bank, Washington, DC.

Deininger, K., H. Selod, and A. Burns. 2012. "The Land Governance Assessment Framework: Identifying and Monitoring Good Practice in the Land Sector." World Bank, Washington, DC.

Ghana Judicial Service. 2010. "Impact Analysis of the Automated Land Courts in Accra." Draft Working Paper, Ghana Judicial Service, Accra.

Huchzermeyer, M. 2008. "Slum Upgrading in Nairobi within the Housing and Basic Services Market: A Housing Rights Concern." *Journal of Asian and African Studies* 43 (1): 19–39.

Kasanga, K., and N. Kotey. 2001. "Land Management in Ghana: Building on Tradition and Modernity." International Institute for Environment and Development, London.

Keith, S., P. McAuslan, R. Knight, J. Lindsay, P. Munro-Faure, and D. Palmer. 2008. *Compulsory Acquisition of Land and Compensation.* FAO Land Tenure Series. Rome: FAO.

Klopp, J. M. 2000. "Pilfering the Public: The Problem of Land Grabbing in Contemporary Kenya." *Africa Today* 47 (1): 7–26.

Kotey, A. 2004. "Final Report: Legislative and Judicial for the Land Administration Project." Ministry of Lands, Forestry and Natural Resources, Accra.

Larbi, W. O., A. Antwi, and P. Olomolaiye. 2004. "Compulsory Land Acquisition in Ghana: Policy and Praxis." *Land Use Policy* 21 (2): 115–27.

Mabogunje, A. L. 1992. "Perspectives on Urban Land and Urban Management Policies in Sub-Saharan Africa." Technical Paper 196, Africa Technical Department, World Bank, Washington, DC.

Memon, P. A. 1982. "The Growth of Low-Income Settlements: Planning Response in the Peri-Urban Zone of Nairobi." *Third World Planning Review* 4 (2): 145–58.

Musyoka, R. 2004. "Informal Land Delivery Processes in Eldoret, Kenya." Policy Brief 3, International Development Department, University of Birmingham, U.K.

Ngau, P., J. Nyabuti, R. Musyoka, and J. Klopp. 2010. "Land-Use Conversion in the Urban-Rural Fringes of Metropolitan Nairobi, Kenya: Dynamics and Issues." Working Paper, World Bank, Washington, DC.

Olima, W. H. A. 1997. "The Conflicts, Shortcomings, and Implications of the Urban Land Management System in Kenya." *Habitat International* 21 (3): 319–31.

Omwenga, M. 2008. "Urban Growth and Sprawl: Case Study of Nairobi, Kenya." Paper presented to the World Urban Forum, Nanjing, November 3–9.

Tanner, C. 2002. "Law Making in an African Context: The 1997 Mozambican Land Law." Legal Papers Online 26, FAO, Paris. http://www.fao.org/Legal/Prs-OL/lpo26.pdf.

Tchale, H. 2012. "Pilot Redistributive Land Reform in Malawi: Innovations and Emerging Good Practices." Working Paper for the "Land Administration and Reform in SSA" study, World Bank, Washington, DC.

Thuo, A. D. M. 2010. "Community and Social Responses to Land Use Transformations in the Nairobi Rural-Urban Fringe, Kenya." *Field Actions Science Report* (special issue 1, February): 1–10.

Torhonen, M. P., and D. Palmer. 2004. "Land Administration in Post-Conflict Cambodia." Paper presented at the symposium, "Post-Conflict Land Administration Areas," Geneva, April 29–30.

United Republic of Kenya. 2001. *Report of the Commission of Inquiry into the Land Law System of Kenya (Njonjo Commission).* Nairobi: Government Printer.

———. 2004. *Report of the Commission of Inquiry into the Illegal/Irregular Allocation of Public Land.* Nairobi: Government Printer.

———. 2008. "Nairobi Metro 2030: A World-Class African Metropolis Nairobi." Government Printer for the Ministry of Nairobi Metropolitan Development, Nairobi.

———. 2009. "Sessional Paper No. 3 of 2009 on National Land Policy, August 2009." Government Printer for the Ministry of Lands, Nairobi.

———. 2010. "The Constitution of Kenya 2010." National Council for Law Reporting, Nairobi.

West, H. W. 1964. "The Mailo System in Buganda: A Preliminary Case Study in African Land Tenure." Government Printer, Entebbe.

World Bank. 2003. "Ghana Land Administration Project." Project Appraisal Document, World Bank, Washington, DC.

———. 2004. "Malawi Community-Based Rural Land Development Project." Project Appraisal Document, World Bank, Washington, DC.

———. 2005. "Uganda Private Sector Competitiveness Project II, Land Component Project Implementation Manual." World Bank, Washington, DC.

———. 2010. "Uses and Users of Justice in Africa: The Case of Ghana's Specialized Courts." Final report submitted to Her Ladyship the Chief Justice of Ghana and the World Bank.

———. 2011a. "Ghana Land Administration Project." Implementation Completion and Results Report, World Bank, Washington, DC.

———. 2011b. "Kenya Informal Settlements Improvement Project." Project Appraisal Document, World Bank, Washington, DC.

———. 2012. "Ghana Commercial Agricultural Project." Project Appraisal Document, World Bank, Washington, DC.

World Resources Institute. 2001. "Uganda: The Compulsory Acquisition of Privately Held Land by Government." World Resources Institute, Washington, DC.

Zimmermann, W. 2002. "Comments on Land in Conflict and Post-Conflict Situations." Paper presented at the World Bank Regional Land Workshop, Phnom Penh, June 4–6.

Chapter 5

Modernizing Infrastructure and Selecting Appropriate and Affordable Technologies for Surveying and Mapping

The basic hardware of land administration is the surveying and mapping infrastructure, providing the skeleton of a spatial framework for recording land rights. To do this efficiently and officially, systems need to incorporate at least two sets of information: (a) registers of largely textual or alphanumeric data that record rights in land and transactions or changes over time and (b) maps or a spatial framework that defines the boundaries and extent of land over which these rights apply. In many developing countries, including those in Sub-Saharan Africa, the spatial frameworks for recording land rights are weak or nonexistent. This typically results in problems such as overlapping claims and disputes over boundaries and can be a major cause of uncertainty in rights to land.

While the main rationale for investing in modern surveying and mapping technologies is to create or strengthen the spatial framework for mitigating these problems, investments in surveying and mapping have other benefits as well. One such benefit is the provision of basic information on the spatial extent of landholdings for government purposes such as land use planning, assessment and collection of land taxes, and management and allocation of public land. Other benefits are derived from the collection of basic information for strategic planning, construction, utilities, communication and transportation (air, sea, and land), exploration and mining, natural resource management, precision agriculture, policing and emergencies, disaster management, administration of local, regional, and international boundaries, and security.

This chapter discusses surveying and mapping in the context of land administration and specifically covers three technological areas of interest for establishing spatial frameworks: geodetic referencing, large-scale base mapping (LSBM), and cadastral surveying, whose costs often constitute more than 50 percent of total investments in land administration projects. Geodetic referencing is the establishment of a coordinate reference system (based on the shape, size, and position of a reference mathematical surface) and its associated infrastructure, such as networks of geodetic control points and procedures that enable features and information on many different themes or topics to be surveyed and mapped. LSBM (that is, a scale sufficient to define or chart cadastral boundaries, typically greater than 1:10,000) provides a spatial framework for a range of land administration purposes, including demarcating land parcel boundaries and other cadastral information and maintaining a record of land parcel boundaries. Cadastral surveying refers to the field and office procedures used to survey and chart land parcel boundaries and other cadastral information, as well as the procedures used to maintain this spatial information.

Inadequate and Inappropriate Past Investments in Surveying and Mapping

Investments and technologies in surveying and mapping in Sub-Saharan Africa have not been adequately evaluated, and this has led to poor investment decisions and lack of accountability:

- High-accuracy cadastral surveys, plans, and maps meant for high-value central business districts and urban lands have been specified for registering low-value regional and rural lands (at excessive cost) in many countries.
- Cadastral and registration systems are incomplete, as governments are unable to fund the high cost of specified procedures, and out of date, as users are not willing to pay the high cost for the surveys necessary to update the records.
- There have been (usually) unsuccessful attempts to produce and maintain countrywide, small-scale topographic mapping series with limited demand and limited technical resources.
- Networks of continuously operating reference stations (CORSs) have been established in an unsustainable manner, without proper consideration for user needs and without sufficient policy and capacity to provide adequate service to government and private users.

At least two factors explain the inadequate scrutiny and appraisal of investments in surveying and mapping technologies in Sub-Saharan Africa. First, these activities are often appraised as part of larger land registration investment packages. This is deceptive, as surveying and mapping typically constitute more than half the cost of a systematic land registration activity. Second, since surveys and mapping are also undertaken for purposes supporting the military, internal security, public administration, or disaster management, technical staff may claim that the expenditures are beyond scrutiny because they serve strategic interests.

In the absence of serious appraisal, surveying and mapping procedures are frequently modeled on Western systems with little regard for local circumstances and difficulties, such as limited capacity, resources, and funding, and the legal requirements for surveying and mapping often diverge widely from actual practice. Further, decisions on technology and investment are often monopolized by technical staff, particularly surveyors, who are biased toward highly precise, accurate, and sophisticated technologies. Lastly, professional associations often exercise political influence to promote laws and regulations that favor high, but sometimes inappropriate, levels of accuracy and technologies that are excessively expensive.

The Need for Technical and Economic Appraisal of Technologies

Before major investments are made to modernize Africa's surveying and mapping infrastructure, both investments and technologies need to be adequately appraised. For policy makers to justify investment in and adoption of new technologies, those technologies must be deemed cost-effective, sustainable, and appropriately tailored to the factors particular to Sub-Saharan Africa:

- Dual systems of land tenure, with a formal system based on a Western model of land administration, typically with limited effectiveness and scope, and a larger, informal system based on custom, often with limited but growing formal recognition
- Limited resources and capacity.

To meet the criteria of low cost and sustainability in Sub-Saharan Africa, the search for technology must go beyond the three core technologies (geodetic referencing, LSBM, and cadastral surveying). For example, global navigational satellite systems (GNSSs) have created new possibilities, with GNSS technology now available in low-cost handheld systems and in vehicle-based navigation systems. Given that GNSS technology is also deployed in a wide range of consumer goods, notably mobile phones and digital cameras, the general population has a great capacity to capture spatial data. In many cases, spatial data are even being gathered without user input (for example, coordinates tagged to a digital camera file). High-resolution satellite imagery is also increasingly available to the public; for example, spatial portals such as Google Earth make data readily available and provide a platform for users to upload and display spatial data.[1] This satellite imagery is already linked to surveying and mapping tools, such as Trimble's Trimble Business Center.[2]

Technical Evaluation

Improvements in GNSSs, LSBM, and geographic information systems have enabled spatial technology to be used for new applications such as participatory or community mapping (IFAD 2009). GNSS and mapping technologies are increasingly being used to map and chart indigenous rights (Poole 1995). For example, the Forest Peoples Program records recent participatory mapping efforts in Cameroon, Guyana, and Uganda.[3] The Rainforest Foundation UK has undertaken participatory mapping in various countries, including Cameroon, the Democratic Republic of Congo, Gabon, and Peru, and has posted online examples of participatory mapping in a range of countries in Africa.[4]

The potential for "crowd sourcing" has been noted in the spatial industry, especially by OpenStreetMap and by TomTom in the maintenance of its navigation database.[5] McLaren (2011) proposes establishing and maintaining land administration data through a crowd-sourcing system, based on the ready availability of mobile phones and cameras with GNSS and open-source software. This innovative approach faces various difficulties in implementation, including authentication of information submitted, resistance from land professionals such as surveyors, and the need for information and communications technology and for technology support. But there is no doubt that crowd sourcing has the potential to collect land rights information to improve land tenure security in a cost-effective and participatory manner; in particular, the spatial data collected using parasurveyors can be used to update base maps and massive cadastral databases such as those recently created by national registration programs in Ethiopia and Rwanda. While appealing, McLaren's approach and the innovative uses of new technology envisioned by Adlington (2011)—for example, vehicle-based laser-induced direction and range (LIDAR), inexpensive and quick aerial photography, handheld GNSS devices, and mobile phones and cameras—have yet to be demonstrated in a practical application. Given their great potential to reduce costs and extend land tenure security to many households in rural areas and urban slums, these new technologies and innovative approaches should be piloted expeditiously and scaled up if they pass the test.

Economic Evaluation

The rapid development of spatial technology has real relevance to Sub-Saharan Africa. However, these technologies and their associated investments need to be subjected to either a cost-benefit or a cost-effectiveness analysis. Conducting a conventional cost-benefit analysis of investments in geodetic networks, LSBM, and cadastral surveying confronts at least two challenges: (a) attribution of benefits, which refers to tracking the appropriate source of benefits, and (b) quantification of benefits once they have been segregated and attributed. Because of these difficulties, cost-effectiveness analysis is more commonly used, as it takes the project's benefits as given and seeks to identify the least-cost means of achieving them. A detailed description of cost-benefit and cost-effectiveness analyses and their application to surveying and mapping technologies and investments can be found in Byamugisha et al. (2012). Table 5.1 shows selected unit cost norms for surveys and mapping that can be used as a reference in cost-effectiveness analysis and for planning and implementing procurement.

In the past, high standards of survey accuracy intended for high-value urban lands were used for registering low-value rural lands in many African countries, at excessive expense. Thus the standards of accuracy should be carefully specified to avoid incurring unnecessarily high costs for registering relatively low-value rural lands. As Dale and McLaughlin (1999) demonstrated, there is an inverse relationship between accuracy and cost (see figure B5.1.1 in box 5.1).

Table 5.1 Unit Cost Norms for Surveying and Mapping Relevant to Sub-Saharan Africa

a. Unit costs of CORSs in select European and African countries

Country	Number of CORSs	Year	Investment cost (US$)	Unit cost (US$)
Macedonia, FYR	14	2007	615,595	43,971
Serbia	34	2004	1,244,000	36,586
Turkey	145	2007–09	4,200,000	29,099
Ethiopia	1	2003	—	36,500
Ghana	5	2007	164,160	32,832
Tanzania	2	2009	—	30,000

b. Unit cost of base mapping

Source of LSBM	Image scale and resolution	Unit costs (US$ per square kilometer)			
		Europe	Ethiopia	Ghana	Tanzania
Satellite imagery; ortho-rectified (new; at least 30 square kilometers)	GeoEye (0.5 meter)	30	30	30	30
Aerial photography (250 square kilometers)	1:45,000 (50-centimeter pixel)	31.5	—	150	—
Line mapping (analog method)	1:2,000	1,643	—	—	—

c. Unit cost of various survey methodologies in Ethiopia

Survey methodology	Cost per parcel (US$)	Survey time or speed per parcel (hours:minutes)
Handheld GPS	4.98	00:19
Rope only	0.81	00:15
Rope and handheld GPS	0.97	00:17
Tape and compass	18.18	01:34
Tape and compass and hand	18.29	01:36
All stations	7.27	00:23
IKONOS satellite imagery	14.23	00:17

Source: Adopted from Byamugisha et al. 2012.
Note: — = not available. CORS = continuously operating reference station. GPS = global positioning system.

BOX 5.1

Accuracy and Cost

Among the technical considerations, the relationship between costs and accuracy has attracted considerable attention. It is captured in figure B5.1, which essentially shows an inverse relationship between the required accuracy and the unit (per parcel) surveying cost.

For every level of accuracy, there are various technological packages with different cost implications. Each of the three curves represents a given package, labeled as technological package 1, 2, or 3. A vertical line cutting these curves (that is, fixing the level of unit cost at a certain level) identifies the curve for technological package 1 as the most cost-effective choice of technology, because it offers the best accuracy for a given level of cost. Similarly, a horizontal line cutting the three curves (that is, fixing the level of accuracy) arrives at the same conclusion via a different route. That is, it identifies the technological package corresponding to the lowest cost for a given level of accuracy. The choice again is technological package 1. This way, too, we can identify the most cost-effective choice of technology.

Figure B5.1.1 Accuracy and Cost Models for Cadastral Surveys

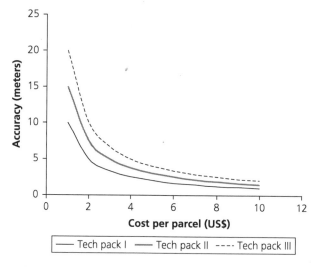

Source: Byamugisha et al. 2012.
Note: Tech pack = technological package. Technological package 1 = satellite imagery; technological package 2 = aerial photography; and technological package 3 = handheld global positioning system with and without differential corrections.

Source: Adapted from Byamugisha et al. 2012.

Modernizing Geodetic Reference Frames

Geodetic reference frames (GRFs) are the prerequisite infrastructure for positioning, geo-referencing, and geo-spatial data technologies, which are themselves essential for supporting the land-based production of goods and services as well as the planning and development of physical infrastructure. They are also the foundation on which the national spatial data infrastructure (NSDI) is built. Unfortunately for most African countries, the GRFs inherited at independence were sparsely populated and nationally isolated (particularly from other countries with different colonial administrators); many were never observed or never adjusted to international standards. While national surveying and mapping departments and military surveyors maintained the old GRFs and updated them as best they could, stations still deteriorated over time, and many of the established monuments were destroyed or vandalized.

After implementation of the African Doppler Survey in the 1980s, African countries started to introduce the World Geodetic System 1984 (WGS-84) geocentric reference system, which has evolved to the modern global positioning system (GPS) standard. To realize synergies and efficiencies within and across countries, countries have been working on the African geodetic reference frame (AFREF). This common fundamental platform will enable efficient generation of geo-referenced products, applications, and services, with implementation at the national level but coordination at a pan-African level. Modernization of GRFs in Sub-Saharan Africa will take advantage of the increased access to

A CORS at Bawjiase, Ghana, Built under the Land Administration Project

Photo credit: ©Isaac Karikari, project coordinator, Land Administration Project, Phase 2, Ghana.

satellite technology, with its declining costs per unit. As of May 2011, 26 countries had established at least one continuously operating reference station, and about 50 CORSs were contributing data to AFREF's Operational Data Center, which started collecting and disseminating spatial data from permanent GNSSs in Africa in June 2010 (Govender 2011). To make AFREF fully operational, each country will establish a fundamental CORS to serve as a permanent AFREF station.

Notwithstanding the progress made, existing geo-data products, including maps, are still based on local coordinate systems and require conversion. Consequently, a typical land administration project in Sub-Saharan Africa involves redefining the national reference frame and datum—a known position from which all height information is relatively measured—establishing GNSS-based GRFs with CORSs, and including GNSS observations to determine or refine detailed transformation parameters from the local coordinate systems to GNSSs. For example, Ghana is replacing its current GRF with one based on WGS-84 using GNSS CORSs, while Ethiopia and Tanzania are replacing theirs with one based on WGS-84, but accessed with a mix of GNSS-based stations and CORSs (see box 5.2). The GNSS-based modern GRF

BOX 5.2

Modernization of GRFs in Ethiopia, Ghana, and Tanzania

The geodetic reference frame modernization programs of three countries give a sense of the direction and content of the ongoing modernization in Sub-Saharan Africa: Ghana is establishing CORSs, Tanzania is using GNSS-based GRF stations, and Ethiopia is applying both. All three countries are forging ahead without a GRF policy on how users might access and pay for data. Capacity building, especially to operate and maintain the modern GRFs, also lags behind the modernization programs.

Established in 1957, Ethiopia's original GRF uses the Adindan datum and the Clarke 1880 ellipsoid (modified). It covers the northern part of the country, including Addis Ababa, although the Ethiopian Mapping Agency has focused on extending and making the control network more dense. In its modernization program and in cooperation with German institutions, the Geophysical Observatory at Addis Ababa University has operated an International GNSS Service (IGS) CORS in the international terrestrial reference frame (ITRF) since 2007. Since 2005, four more CORSs have been established with support from the U.S. Agency for International Development, one IGS-standard station in Addis Ababa, two in the Dire Dawa and Jimma airports, and one in Gonder. The Ethiopian Mapping Agency recently acquired funding from the United Nations Economic Commission for Africa to install a fifth station at Assosa. None of these is linked to AFREF yet.

(continued next page)

Box 5.2 (continued)

Ghana's original GRF used various datums: Accra datum, War Office 1926 ellipsoid, Leigon 1977 datum, and the Clarke 1880 ellipsoid (modified). Under a World Bank–funded Land Administration Project, co-financed by Kreditanstalt für Wiederaufbau, modernization began by establishing a GNSS-based GRF in 2006, and the datum changed to WGS-84. In 2007, five stand-alone CORSs and 28 old points were observed to calculate transformation parameters. The fundamental CORS in Kumasi and the CORS in Accra are to be linked by Internet to AFREF. Three witness markers around the GRF stations facilitate traditional surveys, with total stations to tie in. Under the second phase of the project, about 30 more CORSs will cover the entire country, with interspacing of 70 to 100 kilometers. The new CORS network should be fully established and operational by the end of 2013.

Tanzania's original GRF, which is outdated and sparse, uses the Arc 1960 datum and Clarke 1880 ellipsoid. Under a World Bank–funded private sector competitiveness project, modernization begun in 2009 replaced the old GRF with a modern one linked to the ITRF. This involved the use of high-precision GPS to establish and provide access to a fundamental datum that integrates a zero to second-order GNSS-based GRF, with 13 zero-order stations, 72 first-order stations at approximately 110-kilometer (or 1°) spacing, and about 600 second-order stations with 40-kilometer spacing. The GNSS-based GRF is being supplemented with a small network of CORSs, including a fundamental CORS linked with AFREF, to provide even more efficient, fast, and precise correctional data, especially in denser urban areas. Finally, work on an absolute gravity network is expected to be completed by December 2012.

Source: Adapted from Byamugisha et al. 2012.

---

infrastructure being built offers important advantages for cadastral surveying. Any predefined need for accuracy can be met with the available range of GNSS single- or dual-frequency receivers (rovers) using high-quality GNSS-based GRFs. Surveyors can now work anywhere within reach of a GRF with a uniform minimum level of precision. Basic cadastral survey modes include (a) a real-time kinematic mode, with a rover-base set or within a CORS network, receiving correction data in real time through a radio or a modem, or (b) a postprocessing mode, with corrections introduced later in the office. Both modes rely on GRF access, either a local base station acting as a temporary reference station or a CORS. This significantly reduces the cost of surveying, as a simple handheld GPS (single-frequency) device costs US$200–US$300, while a total-station or dual-frequency differential GPS device costs about US$10,000.

Modernizing the Production of Base Maps and Other Spatial Data

Base mapping can be used for many special or thematic mapping efforts, and in the case of LSBM, one such theme may include the cadastre. This applies to LSBM if the parcels can be identified by boundary features on the base map or image with no further cadastre surveying required. While not a prerequisite for the cadastre, large-scale geo-spatial data in a scale, detail, or resolution that matches the prevailing parcel sizes in the area concerned may be instrumental for cadastral mapping. For example, the Land Registry of England and Wales uses large-scale ordnance survey base topographic maps to identify parcels and compile parcel index maps and title (parcel) plans, without conducting cadastral surveys in the field.

A key problem for the vast majority of African countries is that the fundamental spatial data sets are either not available at all or not available in the form and currency required. For example, in many African countries, the 1:50,000-scale topographic maps that commonly serve as base maps are out of date and in analog form (Kufoniyi 2009). In Ethiopia, Ghana, and Tanzania, most of the 1:50,000-scale maps were compiled more than 40 years ago and are now being updated and digitized with support from development partners. Urban mapping (at scale of 1:2,500) has been undertaken recently in these countries, but much of the effort has focused on central parts of the city, with very limited coverage of periurban areas (see box 5.3). There is a need to scale up investments both to produce new maps and to update old ones to meet user requirements. When assessing the technology and investment choices, the focus should be on building a fit-for-purpose framework that meets the needs of society today and can be incrementally improved over time (see Enemark 2012).

Cadastral Surveying and Mapping

Cadastral surveying and mapping are technical processes that officially record the spatial location or extent of land rights that have typically been adjudicated and demarcated in the field. There is great variety in the cadastral surveying options, in terms of both accuracy and cost. Options include sketch maps, using GNSS to map centroids, and accurate but expensive ground surveys. In the developed world, well-established cadastral systems have strong support from government and private sector actors such as cadastral surveyors; they also have support from the general public. In the developing world, the major issue is deciding on the appropriate strategy and approach to take in gathering the textual and spatial data that record rights in land and then establishing systems to maintain the data.

Tattered Cadastral Map in the Kampala Land Registry, Uganda, before Repair and Scanning and Reproduction Using a New Base Map

a. Before repair and scanning

b. Reproduction using a new base map

Photo credit: ©Richard Oput, land component coordinator, Second Private Sector Competitiveness Project, Uganda.

Major first-registration (or land titling) projects have tended to adopt a mapping base for the spatial framework due to economies of scale. Where occupation is clearly visible from the sky, large-scale orthophoto maps produced using either aerial photography or high-resolution satellite imagery can be very useful for charting both fixed and general boundaries. In Rwanda, a major land tenure

BOX 5.3

Modernization of Base Mapping and Other Spatial Data in Ethiopia, Ghana, and Tanzania

The Ethiopian Mapping Agency is mandated to produce topographic maps and related spatial data. It earlier produced topographic maps of the country and is currently producing a series of 1:50,000-scale maps, the standard topographic map in the country (1,580 map sheets provide about 85 percent coverage). These maps are about 30 years old. As part of the modernization program, some maps are being digitized, but most are still in analog form. Urban maps (1:2,000 scale) exist in analog form for major cities. The plan is to digitize all maps and continue producing digital maps in the future.

In Ghana, the Surveying and Mapping Division of the Land Commission is mandated to provide maps and other geo-information: 1:2,500-scale maps cover cities and towns, and 1:50,000-scale maps provide national coverage. The latter comprise 351 map sheets, suitable for recording boundaries of Stool land, but most are out of date, as they were compiled from aerial photography acquired from 1966 to 1974. Under a project sponsored by the Japan International Cooperation Agency (JICA), 40 sheets of the 1:50,000-scale maps, covering 25,000 square kilometers over southwestern Ghana, including Accra and Tema, were revised. The World Bank–supported Land Administration Project (Phases 1 and 2) has supported production of LSBM suitable for registering land at 1:5,000 and 1:2,500 map scales. Most cities and towns, including Accra-Tema and Kumasi, have been mapped at 1:2,500 scale under various projects, but some are outdated.

In Tanzania, the Surveying and Mapping Division of the Ministry of Lands, Housing, and Human Settlement Development is responsible for producing and disseminating maps and other spatial data. The 1:50,000-scale maps provide basic coverage of the whole country; there are about 1,626 topographic sheets, mostly compiled in the 1970s. In 1994–95, 34 map sheets were published using aerial photography from 1992. Tanzania's outdated maps are being partially updated, digitized, and vectorized (scanned) with donor support from JICA and the World Bank. Limited 1:10,000- and 1:25,000-scale maps cover only six districts. Urban scale mapping (1:2,500) has been undertaken recently (1:5,000 for townships) using aerial photogrammetry, but is mostly confined to central city areas, with very limited periurban coverage. The Surveying and Mapping Division produces the maps from about 800 stereomodels a year using outdated equipment under the National Urban Mapping Program, which covers about 2,000 square kilometers (20–30 townships) each year. Most urban maps are older than 5 years, and some 70 percent of the maps are more than 20 years old.

Source: Byamugisha et al. 2012.

regularization project has charted all of the nearly 10.5 million land parcels in the country using large-scale orthophoto maps as a spatial framework. Where it is problematic to identify visually the boundaries on the imagery, supplementary ground survey techniques are required. These can be GNSS or total-station techniques; in rural areas, they can even be inexpensive handheld GPS measurements or even tapes in some circumstances.

Recent large-scale topographic maps, particularly photomaps, can greatly facilitate the generation of a spatial framework. The large-scale topographic maps prepared for military purposes by Ordnance Survey in the United Kingdom provided the basis for the spatial framework for land titles in that country. Where large-scale mapping is not available, a large budget and a long time frame have traditionally been required to produce the necessary base mapping, although this is changing with improved systems and increased competition for supply of high-resolution satellite imagery. Simple handheld GPS equipment has been used in some countries (including Ethiopia and Tanzania) but suffers from several difficulties, including limited accuracy (5–8 meters) and relatively high investment in building capacity to capture and maintain the map data.

On the whole, there is no universal survey or mapping solution or recipe for success. Each individual set of circumstances requires well-tailored solutions. What is appropriate in a densely populated, high-rise city center will not make sense in an arid rural area with traditional transhumant pastoralism. Against this background, a few lessons can be drawn from experiences in Sub-Saharan Africa and elsewhere:

- Systematic cadastral surveys (for all parcels in a defined larger area) are more cost-efficient than sporadic ones (for a single parcel responding to an application from an individual) due to economies of scale. They are also more transparent, as the process is typically implemented with strong community involvement and oversight and the adjudication material is usually publicly displayed in the community, with a process to record and address disputed claims.

- Critical cost savings in cadastral surveying can be realized by choosing reasonable levels of accuracy and precision to describe the parcels, leading to affordable survey technology. Given that a cadastral survey does not necessarily require high accuracy and precision to provide secure tenure or transfer of rights, high-accuracy surveys may not be necessary unless used for land of high value.

- Large-scale aerial orthophoto maps can provide a cost-effective spatial framework for programs of land registration that cover a region or a country, as they did recently in Rwanda.

Notes

1. http://www.google.com/earth/index.html.
2. http://www.trimble.com/survey/trimble-business-center.aspx.
3. http://www.forestpeoples.org/topics/environmental-governance/ participatory-resource-mapping.
4. http://www.rainforestfoundationuk.org/Projects; http://www.mappingforrights.org.
5. http://www.openstreetmap.org.

References

Adlington, G. 2011. "The Rise or Fall of the Cadastre Empire." Presentation at the seventh Annual Meeting and International Symposium "Cadastre 2.0," International Federation of Surveyors, Innsbruck, Austria, September 25–October 1.

Byamugisha, F. F. K., T. Burns, V. Evtimov, S. Satana, and G. Zulsdorf. 2012. "Appraising Investments and Technologies for Surveying and Mapping for Land Administration in Sub-Saharan Africa." Working Paper for the "Land Administration and Reform in SSA" study, World Bank, Washington, DC.

Dale, P., and J. McLaughlin. 1999. *Land Administration.* Oxford: Oxford University Press.

Enemark, S. 2012. "Sustainable Land Governance: Spatially Enabled, Fit for Purpose, and Supporting the Global Agenda." Paper presented at the Annual Conference, "Land and Poverty," World Bank, Washington, DC, April 23–26.

Govender, S. 2011. "Report of the Committee on Development, Information, Science, and Technology." United Nations Economic Commission for Africa, Addis Ababa.

IFAD (International Fund for Agricultural Development). 2009. "Good Practices in Participatory Mapping." Report prepared for IFAD, Rome.

Kufoniyi, O. 2009. "Of Road Blocks and Building Blocks." *GIS Development Global Magazine* (special issue on Africa, July). Noida, India.

McLaren, R. A. 2011. "Crowd-Sourcing Support of Land Administration: A New, Collaborative Partnership between Citizens and Land Professions." RICS Research, Royal Charter of Institutional Surveyors, Brussels.

Poole, P. 1995. "Indigenous Peoples, Mapping, and Biodiversity Conservation: An Analysis of Current Activities and Opportunities for Applying Geomatics Technologies." Biodiversity Support Program, Landover, MD.

Chapter 6

Modernizing Systems and Developing Capacities

This study focuses on land administration, specifically on security of land tenure, but other elements within land administration also have to be addressed to pave the way toward sustainable land governance. In this chapter, important themes of systems, functions, and capacity development are discussed in the context of land administration, highlighting challenges and opportunities for modernization and for scale-up of past initiatives. These include the following:

- Developing computerized land information systems and national spatial data infrastructure
- Decentralizing land administration to empower local communities and traditional authorities
- Strengthening valuation functions and land tax policies to raise revenue efficiently and fairly for cost recovery and decentralized governance
- Strengthening land use planning and regulations for sustainable development
- Reforming institutions and developing capacity for land administration and management.

Developing Computerized Land Information Systems

National spatial data infrastructure (NSDI) plays an important role in coordinating efforts to develop land information systems (LISs) and to integrate land information with other spatial data. Development of both LISs and NSDI has been a slow process in Sub-Saharan Africa, although it has accelerated in recent years. This section reviews recent experience with developing computerized LISs and NSDI with a view to deriving lessons for scaling up efforts across the continent.

Land administration systems in many African countries are characterized by time-consuming, inefficient, and expensive procedures; lack of transparency; corruption; low public confidence; and generally insecure transactions. As noted in chapter 1, in 2011 it took an average of 65 days to transfer an already registered property in Sub-Saharan Africa compared to only 31 days in Organisation for Economic Co-operation and Development (OECD) countries (World Bank 2011a). To address the inefficiencies and other problems in land administration, many African countries have initiated programs to computerize land registries and establish land information systems.[1] For example, Ghana and Uganda plan to make computerized LISs a cornerstone of their land administration and management systems, with support from World Bank–funded projects (World Bank 2003, 2004b, 2011d).

The expected benefits of properly implemented land information systems for governments, businesses, and society include increased security of land titles and land transactions with significantly reduced time for such transactions; greater transparency and traceability of land transactions; a reduction in fraud, informal arrangements, and corruption in the sector; more timely, accurate, and reliable information about land resources and their quantity, quality, ownership, and use for evidence-based decision making; and increased public confidence in the land administration system. Evidence from India indicates that computerization of land records can also lead to increased access to credit (Deininger and Goyal 2012). According to the World Bank (2011a), 27 economies that computerized their registries in the past seven years cut the average time to transfer property in half, by about three months. The increase in revenue collection and reduction in corruption can be considerable as well. The Indian state of Karnataka, notwithstanding a cut in stamp duty from 14 percent to 8 percent, quadrupled its land-related revenue from US$120 million in 2000 to US$480 million in 2005 as a result of computerizing land registration and improving property valuation; the computerization saved users US$16 million in bribes (Deininger 2008).

Although Ghana and Uganda have only partially computerized, they are already reaping benefits from computerization and related reforms. For example, Ghana cut the average time to transfer property from 169 days in 2005 to 34 days in 2011, although a considerable part of the impact came from decentralizing its deeds registry to 10 regional centers. It also increased its annual land-related revenue from US$12 million in 2003 to US$135 million in 2010, more than a tenfold increase, while keeping the average total cost of registration as a share of property value at 0.7 percent (World Bank 2011a, 2011d). Uganda cut the average time to transfer property from 227 days in 2007 to 48 days in 2011 by combining computerization with rehabilitation of manual land registries and other reforms, especially in property valuation (World Bank 2011a).

While computerization and development of LISs generate considerable benefits, the vast majority of developing countries still rely on paper-based systems and obsolete routines of land registration: more than 80 percent of Sub-Saharan African and South Asian countries still have paper-based systems that are in deteriorated conditions, while 61 percent of the other world economies, including almost all Central Asian, Eastern European, and OECD (high-income) economies, have an electronic database for encumbrances (World Bank 2011a).

Land Records in Uganda's Land Registry before and during Sorting for Computerization

a. Before sorting

b. During sorting

Photo credit: ©Richard Oput, land component coordinator, Second Private Sector Competitiveness Project, Uganda.

Benefits from computerization are not quickly realized. Programs for computerization and LISs can take up to 10 years to develop and require considerable financial resources and capacity building (McLaren 2011). LISs are technologically and institutionally complex systems that include legally sensitive and economically important information, such as land titles and cadastral data; appropriate security measures are needed to protect data and ensure reliability of the system. The spatial framework for land records and LISs is a fundamental data set in a spatial data infrastructure (SDI), and it is therefore important that the LIS and the survey, maps, and imagery used to prepare the LIS are compatible with SDI policies and standards (on matters such as unique parcel identifiers, data formats and accuracy, metadata, and data exchange and sharing).

Best practices gleaned from computerization experiences in seven Indian states[2] include (a) reengineering business processes, (b) involving the private sector through outsourcing or private-public partnerships, (c) collecting user fees to achieve fiscal sustainability, and (d) first computerizing in areas with high volumes of land transactions and gradually extending coverage to areas with low transactions (World Bank 2007). Additional best-practice elements drawn from global experience include the need to (a) create a land policy and legal framework to guide computerization and LISs and (b) invest significantly in capacity building (McLaren 2011).

Within Sub-Saharan Africa, LIS programs in Ghana and Uganda offer both lessons and best practices:

- Establishment of an LIS requires a systematic approach, detailed system design, and careful planning of each phase.
- Design and implementation of the LIS and the associated activities are best done as a self-contained program or project within a wider program of land administration reform, not as discrete activities of a project.
- An expert with global experience is required to supervise project implementation, similar to the practice in the building and construction industries.
- Free/libre/open-source software (FLOSS) versus commercial off-the-shelf software should be chosen based on software maintenance, license payment, system security, and local capacity to operate the system.
- System design should include document and workflow management components in addition to spatial and textual data to ensure system security and transparency.
- LIS project design should include the rehabilitation and conversion of existing land records to digital form and the integration of base maps with land records.
- Donor support is critical to ensure adequate resources not only for testing different approaches but also for scaling up successful ones.
- LIS development should be part of a broader agenda not only of reform for the land sector but also of reform for public services (see box 6.1 for the approaches taken by Ghana and Uganda).

BOX 6.1

LIS Development in Ghana and Uganda: Piecemeal Versus Comprehensive Approaches

Ghana's LIS was developed around 2005 to address immediate problems, achieve quick wins, and integrate at the end. It opted for homegrown open-source system software to avoid annual licensing fees. Financing was primarily from the World Bank (World Bank 2003). Several activities started concurrently: design and development of LIS for the Greater Accra pilot area, the land use planning management information system (LUPMIS) pilot, the urban management land information system (UMLIS), the land valuation system, and intelligent document scanning of land records. The LIS for the Greater Accra pilot area, completed in 2011, was designed with independent sub-systems for land registration, surveying and mapping, vested and public lands management, and valuation and will be incorporated in a Food and Agriculture Organization of the United Nations (FAO) pilot based on FLOSS. The beta version of the system of land administration (SOLA) software was released in April 2012 and will be further customized to local conditions. An all-embracing architecture is planned for an integrated LIS that will be decentralized to cover all of Ghana's regional centers and be linked to, but not integrated with, the UMLIS and LUPMIS systems.

Potential quick wins included the use of scanned data, separate systems such as UMLIS and LUPMIS, and subsystems for registration, valuation, surveying and mapping, and vested and public lands management, all developed before the integrated LIS. An important challenge to future integration is coordination in systems development and a risk that some systems and subsystems might not communicate easily. Global experience indicates that additional effort and resources will be required to achieve this because appropriate, detailed design and other measures were not taken up-front. FLOSS and the SOLA software, if successfully undertaken, will reduce the dependency on licensed software, but significant effort will be required to customize the design of LIS and system architecture, integrate the system with other components required for land registration and cadastral procedures, and reengineer business processes. Early impacts include (a) a decrease in the average time to transfer property from 169 days in 2005 to 34 days in 2011 and (b) an increase in land-related revenue from US$12 million in 2003 to US$135 million in 2010.

Uganda's LIS initiative is a comprehensive, integrated program to be implemented in a pilot phase and a rollout phase, informed by a baseline study and conceptual design done in 2007–08. The three-year pilot (based in six regional offices holding about 80 percent of all registered land titles in Uganda) was linked to and complemented by a legal review, rehabilitation of land offices, and comprehensive capacity building supported by the World Bank (World Bank 2005c). The seven main components of the pilot (completed in February 2013) are reengineering workflows and processes; designing a detailed system; developing and customizing LIS software;

(continued next page)

Box 6.1 (continued)

reconstructing the geodetic network and producing base maps to anchor and geo-reference the rehabilitation of land and cadastral records; digitizing manual records; integrating and uploading land registry, cadastral records, and spatial data; and implementing all of these in select areas with necessary hardware and software, training, and public awareness campaigns. The pilot also includes (a) establishing a National Land Information Centre as the main national provider of land information and LIS maintenance and support and (b) developing a strategy and a detailed plan to expand LIS coverage nationwide.

Uganda's comprehensive approach was designed to be all-inclusive and therefore avoided the risk of future miscommunication between systems or subsystems. But because it did not prioritize quick wins, it has faced pressure from political leaders. Some of the early impacts include (a) a decrease in the average time to transfer property from 227 days in 2007 to 48 days in 2011, (b) a reduction in the time to process a mortgage from several weeks to 3 days, and (c) a decrease in the time to complete a search on an encumbered title from 15 days to 1.

Source: Adapted from Cheremshynskyi 2012.

Developing National Spatial Data Infrastructure

Spatial data infrastructure is a term that has evolved in recent decades to describe the fundamental spatial data sets and the policies, technologies, standards, criteria, arrangements, and people that enable them to be acquired, processed, maintained, and disseminated throughout all levels of government, the private and nonprofit sectors, and academia. It is driven by the need to produce spatial data once and to use it many times, thereby removing duplication and saving money. Therefore, the discovery, sharing, and dissemination of data are the keys to its success. The spatial framework for land records is the most fundamental data set (layer) needed to make an SDI work (Williamson et al. 2010).

Global experience in formulating and implementing NSDI has generated various lessons and guiding principles that can assist African countries establishing their own NSDI. The most notable are the following (GIC/ESRI Canada 2011):

- There should be a strong business case for SDI.
- Legislation is a strong enabler of SDI.

- Existing structures and institutional arrangements should be built upon.
- All stakeholders should remain engaged.
- The focus should initially be on specific areas of application, even while beginning to build longer-term, generic architecture.
- SDI implementation can take a long time (often more than five years) to produce outcomes, and attention should be paid to gaining momentum and to ensuring sustainability of implementation through successive smaller "quick wins."
- A mitigation plan for technological challenges during early phases of SDI development should be developed.
- Poor handover and lack of continuity (after project closure) are often the cause of SDI failure after donor assistance is withdrawn.

Much attention has been paid to the development of SDI in Africa through the efforts of the United Nations Economic Commission for Africa's Committee on Development Information, Subcommittee on Geo-Information.[3] However, SDI development is progressing very slowly at national levels and appears to have limited political support and inadequate participation by stakeholders. The fundamental data sets either are not available at all or are not available in the form and currency required (see chapter 5). While lack of availability of spatial data is a real concern, availability should not be confused with accuracy; the latter is not critical for the development of SDI. It is therefore important that high standards of accuracy and the associated high costs not be imposed on major initiatives to establish spatial frameworks for land records as the first layer of SDI. International experience has found that spatial frameworks for land records have generally been established under processes that seek to expand coverage as extensively and as quickly as possible, even if this means compromising the accuracy of the spatial information. However, programs to improve the accuracy of spatial frameworks have generally been implemented over time in response to clear user needs rather than as major jurisdiction-wide programs. These can be undertaken as SDI is being developed or even after its completion.

A recent review of Kenya's initiative to establish NSDI found that, after 10 years and considerable expense, the only notable achievement was the development of NSDI standards; neither an NSDI policy nor legislation has been officially adopted, and problems with sharing spatial data persist (see box 6.2). Kenya's experience highlights that, among other things, formulating and implementing an NSDI program can be a long-term venture. It also shows that Kenya could have benefited from the lessons and guiding principles derived from global experience.

BOX 6.2

Development of NSDI in Kenya

In 2001 Kenya embarked on establishing an NSDI by holding a national workshop of representatives of key public and private institutions involved in either producing or using spatial data. An NSDI policy was adopted by stakeholders in August 2009, but as of April 2012 it had not been adopted by the government, nor had legislation been passed to legalize and institutionalize spatial data sharing. Producers and users of spatial data in Kenya still face serious problems in data sharing, as manifested in the duplication of data production efforts and lack of accessibility. The only tangible achievement so far has been the production of NSDI standards and the digitization of manuals and guidelines.

Between 2001 and 2006, five stakeholder workshops led to agreement on the establishing of NSDI and on its process, objectives, structure, rules, and responsibilities. In 2002 stakeholders agreed to launch the NSDI initiative to facilitate the capture, storage, conveyance, and display of geographic information. Survey of Kenya—the country's surveying and mapping organization—was nominated to be the secretariat and implementing agency of the NSDI initiative, which would be funded by the government, public-private partnerships, public investments, and development partners. The NSDI's organizational structure has an executive committee, a steering committee, and four working groups (technical task forces on standards and on legal, education, and dissemination issues). In October 2006 a two-year project funded by the Japan International Cooperation Agency (JICA) launched three main activities: developing NSDI standards, enhancing competence in digitization, and developing resources for NSDI dissemination.

A study covering the period 2002 to 2010 reached the following conclusions regarding the status of Kenya's NSDI (Oloo 2011):

- Standards are the only notable component developed to date.
- The access network is lagging behind, with no clearinghouse for data.
- Most spatial data are still in analog form, and metadata are missing.
- Staff capacity and other organizational aspects have not been developed.
- Stakeholder adoption of an NDSI policy was a major achievement, but delayed approval by the government is a major concern.

Source: Oloo 2011; Murage, Gitimu, and Sato 2008.

Decentralizing Land Administration to Empower Local Communities and Traditional Authorities

Decentralization is recommended when local institutions have a better understanding of local needs and are more inclined to respond to them, as they have better access to information and are more easily held accountable to local populations (Ribot 2001; Sikor and Muller 2009).[4] Given that land is ineffably local, the justification for decentralizing land administration is potentially strong; indeed, in much of Africa, land administration is effectively decentralized to traditional authorities who administer land under custom, with or without a legal foundation in national law. In light of the growing international demand for land and the urgent need to provide written records of land rights to rural people, efforts to decentralize are timely.

The extent to which the benefits of decentralized administration of land are realized depends on how the process is structured and implemented; local governments are not necessarily more democratic, more efficient, or less corrupt than central governments, and not all land administration functions are best carried out at the local level. Centralized management may be needed to deliver technology, maintain uniform national standards, or ensure quality of services. Local capacity may be difficult to create, or the technology needed may be too complex or expensive to maintain locally. Decentralization requires strategies appropriate to the tasks, objectives, and budget. Recent experience suggests that the cost of creating local capacities is high; relying on traditional authorities, who, by and large, still retain considerable popular legitimacy and still control land in much of rural Africa, may be less costly (Bruce and Knox 2009). But the legitimacy of traditional authorities is also eroding rapidly due to pressure from a recent surge in foreign direct investment, significant demand for land for large-scale agriculture, and associated opportunities for corruption (Nolte 2012). No one model or process can ensure success, but a review of what has and has not worked can guide the design of future decentralization.

Bruce and Knox (2009) found that efforts to decentralize authority over land in Africa tend to adopt one of four basic strategies: (a) replicating locally, with some simplification, existing offices of the central government's land agency and granting them limited administrative autonomy; (b) creating more modest and more locally representative specialized bodies at the community level, such as community land boards or committees; (c) decentralizing authority over land to nonspecialized local civil authorities, such as local councils, possibly with the creation of a subcommittee or other subsidiary unit for handling land matters; or (d) relying on traditional authorities as the lowest rung of land administration. Some countries adopt a combination of these, but usually one basic thrust is discernible.

Ethiopia, Ghana, Tanzania, and Uganda have taken different approaches to decentralization. The following subsections review the effectiveness of each, examining (a) the decentralization of land administration roles and who performs them; (b) the interactions of decentralized land administration institutions and those at higher levels; (c) the interactions of decentralized land administration institutions and other local institutions, particularly those with

a role in land management; (d) the extent to which the decentralization decon-
centrates or devolves authority; and (e) the sustainability of each system in management and financial terms. Table 6.1 provides an overview.

Tenure Policy and Legal Context

Ghana and Uganda have strong private property systems with extensive areas
under legally recognized customary land tenure, and traditional institutions
still play important roles in land at the grassroots level. Harmonization of statutory and customary rights and institutions is thus an important consideration
in their programs. In Ethiopia and Tanzania, land markets are restricted by
law, and land use planning is a much stronger motivation than in Ghana and
Uganda. Control of land use and land distribution is an important objective.

**Table 6.1   Key Elements of Land Administration Decentralization Programs in Four African
Countries**

Element	Ethiopia	Ghana	Tanzania	Uganda
Tenure policy and legal context	Statutory rights less than ownership recognized and registrable; limited land marketability	Private ownership and customary rights recognized and registrable; active land markets	Statutory rights less recognized and registrable than ownership rights; limited land marketability	Private ownership and customary rights recognized and registrable; active land markets
Roles decentralized and institutions enabled	Registration and updates of records of land rights to local government and community levels	Registration and updates of records of land rights to local government level	Registration and updates of records of land rights to local government and community levels	Registration and updates of records of land rights to local government level
Deconcentration or devolution of land administration functions	Deconcentration: extension of central government land administration system	Deconcentration: extension of central government land administration system	Deconcentration: extension of central government land administration system	Deconcentration: extension of central government land administration system
Interaction with local land management institutions	New land administration capacity created in local land management institutions, empowering them	New land administration capacity created outside traditional authorities; unclear links to new local land management institutions	New land administration capacity created in local land management institutions, empowering them	New land administration capacity created outside traditional authorities; unclear links to new local land management institutions
Financial sustainability	Cost sharing unclear, no provision for retention of revenues	Cost sharing unclear, no provision for retention of revenues	Cost sharing unclear, no provision for retention of revenues	Cost sharing unclear, no provision for retention of revenues
Social sustainability	Potential increased by decentralizing land administration and management functions to same local institution	Potential for unclear connections to local land management authorities to limit sustainability	Potential increased by decentralizing land administration and management functions to same local institution	Potential for unclear connections to local land management authorities to limit sustainability

Ethiopia and Tanzania have broken the hold of traditional authorities over land and replaced it with civil community-level institutions. Ethiopia and Tanzania do not recognize customary land rights as such, but they do recognize and protect possession.

Decentralization

In Ghana and Uganda, decentralization involves the reform and rehabilitation of weak land registration systems and their extension to more local levels, with the objective being to improve the administration of lands under custom. In both countries, the roles of local traditional and civil authorities seem to be changing. In Uganda, land policy and law call for gradually replacing traditional authorities with local civil land governance institutions, but the actual situation is mixed; the decentralization program has done little to strengthen the new local land governance institutions. The land administration system is being extended to rural areas in a service provision mode, alongside but not well integrated with local land governance institutions. Ghana places the same emphasis on decentralization of registry offices to provide better documentation of customary land rights, with no evidence that customary rights are to be altered. Customary land secretariats (CLSs) have been established by the government to facilitate traditional land administration, but they are the bottom rung of the system. As in Uganda, they provide land administration services to customary landholders, including traditional authorities, whose roles in land governance are largely unchanged. In time, however, as the databases created in the local land registries provide the government with information needed to take over more direct administration of customary land, the role of traditional authorities may decline.

In Ethiopia and Tanzania, strong civil local authorities have a considerable role in identifying rights-holders and their holdings and in recommending the documentation of rights. In both countries, community-level institutions participate substantially in implementation, facilitating the update of registry information. These local institutions also have important roles in land use planning and allocation, as they know when transfers of land take place and are well enough integrated into the overall national system of land governance to be held accountable.

In all four countries, it is clear that the new land registry systems will operate on a far more decentralized basis than they do today. While this decentralization is essentially a "deconcentration" of land administration functions, it does have the potential to enhance community-level land management where these functions are decentralized to the same institutions, as in Ethiopia and Tanzania. In Ghana and Uganda, decentralization of land administration may not empower local land institutions in the same fashion, given the disconnect between land administration and management.

Financial and Social Sustainability

The survey technology being employed in the new systems will be fairly expensive to maintain, and it is unclear how the operating costs will be allocated between central and more local levels of government. While stamp duties on land transactions are common in Sub-Saharan Africa, many African countries have been reluctant to impose land taxes. Excessive reliance on fees for services may drive land users out of the system and into more informal arrangements. Clear fiscal responsibilities are essential for the sustainability of these systems, as the allocation of costs will influence both perceptions of "ownership" and the relative influence of different levels of government on the systems' operations.

The sustainability of decentralized land administration in these four countries will also depend on the buy-in of landholders. Records created at great expense will become quickly outdated unless land users are motivated to register transfers and successions. Education and sensitization of the public and prioritization of the creation of functional registry offices coincident with the initial registrations are part of the solution, but landholders must also see an improvement in tenure security. This is an issue in Ethiopia, where important legal limits are placed on land markets and on the use of land as collateral for loans. In addition, land is subject to reallocation under certain conditions and can be taken if left idle for three years. While impact studies have shown that certification of landholdings in Ethiopia has had a positive impact on investment (Deininger, Ali, and Alemu 2011), there is a risk that continued restrictions on property rights could undermine the sustainability of decentralized formal land administration systems. Ironically, Ethiopia's history of reallocations may foster a stronger appreciation for any increment in tenure security provided by certification and generate a stronger willingness of rights-holders to support system maintenance.

Key Factors for Successful Decentralization

From these experiences, nine factors condition the decision to decentralize land administration in Sub-Saharan Africa:

- Decentralization of land administration happens within the more general decentralization of government and public services. The latter provides a framework for cost sharing by different levels of government, but because the framework is independent of the structure of land administration, it is difficult to find financial information in the project's documentation or indeed any analysis of fiscal sustainability.

- Decentralization can be greatly facilitated if capable community institutions exist. Where traditional authorities still handle most local land governance, feasibility depends on a variety of factors, including the authorities' receptivity and probity. It may be necessary to build competence in local government, a daunting task. In some countries, such as Botswana and Niger, hybrid local land committees include both traditional and civil authorities, suggesting the need for a continuum of approaches.

- Decentralization of land administration tasks tends to deconcentrate central government authority, partly reflecting the desire to facilitate the functioning of national land markets. When the land administration function is decentralized to local institutions with important roles in land management, decentralization can empower those roles as well.

- Land administration systems established through systematic survey and adjudication of rights often experience problems with sustainability due to landholders' failure to register transfers and successions, often due to the high relative costs of registration (Deininger and Feder 2009). Sustainability also suffers when local land management authorities feel isolated from or undermined by the creation of local registries unconnected with them; thus, establishing a clear relationship between those developing and those using registries is critical.

- Initial decentralization of sophisticated land administration machinery requires a strong central government lead and assistance to communities, although a regional or district lead may suffice for very simple systems. There is thus an important link between decentralization and the choice of survey and other technologies.

- Community institutions have an important role to play in maintaining and operating the decentralized system, even when the central government takes a strong lead, especially in the initial identification of holdings and rights-holders; for example, communities can manually maintain primary registers to keep records up to date, although a "culture of registration" must be cultivated.

- The institutional framework for decentralized land administration should be planned conservatively, with a clear sense of the long-term costs of maintaining the system and the source of funding them. Although donor funding is available to create these systems, maintenance and operational costs will ultimately need to be met by domestic resources. Likewise, the availability of donor funding should not encourage governments to opt for technologies that will be too expensive to maintain in the long run.

- Legally imposed rigidity should be avoided in two respects: (a) laws providing for the institutional framework should not specify the technologies and staffing required, as technology changes rapidly, and staffing depends on local needs and capacity, and (b) shared use of a registry by two or more administrative units may be sensible in the early development of the institutions, so laws should allow flexibility in the specification of registries for various administrative levels.

• In light of the growing international demand for land, there is an urgent need to recognize and document the rights of rural people. Among the four countries considered here, only Ethiopia, with its very rough identification of parcels without a sketch or map, can respond to this massive need inexpensively and in a timely fashion. Rwanda uses a similar approach but charts parcels on a photomap (Ali, Deininger, and Goldstein 2011).

Strengthening Valuation Functions and Land Tax Policies to Raise Revenue Efficiently and Fairly for Cost Recovery and Decentralized Governance

Taxes on land and real property provide an effective mechanism to support decentralization of governance in a way that minimizes distortions to the economy while contributing to cost recovery in land administration and discouraging the speculative accumulation of land (Bird and Slack 2004; Brueckner 2000; UN-Habitat, GLTN 2011). But to be effective, efficient, and equitable, land-related taxation must be accompanied by adequate land records and valuation services. Appropriate tax policy must be in place to give local governments the authority to establish tax rates for various classes of property and the capacity to administer tax collection.

While land tax policy and administration are well established in developed countries, they are still weak in African countries. Consequently, many donor-supported land projects and programs in Sub-Saharan Africa contain one or more elements of land tax policy and administration. For example, two successive land projects in Ghana have supported decentralization and strengthening of land registration and valuation functions, revaluation of properties, and studies on land-related taxes to strengthen land-related revenue and cost recovery over nearly 10 years (World Bank 2003, 2011d). This has contributed to impressive increases in annual revenue. Ongoing private sector development projects (with land components) in Tanzania and Uganda (World Bank 2004b, 2005b) are supporting capacity building in property valuation and development of LISs, while the World Bank is providing analytical and advisory services to Madagascar, Malawi, and Mozambique (World Bank 2004a, 2011e, 2011f). With the exception of Ghana, the results in Sub-Saharan Africa have been slow to come, especially in Malawi and Mozambique.

Asian countries have achieved better results, notwithstanding the fact that their land tax policy and administration still need to overcome weaknesses in property valuation and high tax rates that lead to underdeclaration and nonparticipation in land registration (Lunnay 2005). For example, Thailand increased its annual transaction-based, land-related revenue from less than US$200 million in 1984 to US$1.2 billion in 1996 as a result of strengthening land registration and valuation functions under its 20-year Land Titling Program (Brits, Grant, and Burns 2002).[5] Karnataka's success is another example. More recently, the Philippines has gained international recognition for dramatic achievements in increasing land-related revenue within five years by improving four fundamental functions: (a) a spatial property database that is kept up to date (with data provided through the central land agency and augmented by the local government); (b) a mass appraisal process that is consistent with the International Valuation Standard and based on real market transactions; (c) a computerized tax collection system that is integrated with the property database, the valuation database, and the actual payments database; and (d) a tax policy process that includes tax modeling, tax efficiency and compliance reporting, transparency, and the engagement of many stakeholders (see box 6.3).

BOX 6.3

Strengthening Land-Related Revenue in the Philippines

In 2006 the Philippines launched a project co-financed by the World Bank and AusAID to improve land administration and management services and increase land-related revenue via (a) land registration, (b) property valuation and taxation, and (c) local government land and land-related revenue systems strengthened through the Innovation Support Fund (World Bank 2005a). The project's success was fairly unique, especially since previous land administration projects had not been successful in tackling weak property valuation and adversely high tax rates (Lunnay 2005).

The Philippines has a progressive local government code, but local revenue generation is generally weak and dependence on central government allocations is high. Interventions to strengthen local revenues, such as tax mapping and computerization projects, have had limited success, and increases in property value were not being captured through taxation, primarily due to the weak and fragmented land administration system and the lack of inter- and intra-governmental sharing of land information and knowledge. Integrating the land administration and local revenue function reforms was a new approach that involved (a) issuing the first national standard on property valuation; (b) issuing a well-tested procedural manual on mass appraisal for assessors and producing a full set of training materials for standardized instruction; (c) deploying database systems to manage land administration spatial data and property valuation data and to interface with tax collection and geographic information systems (GISs);

(continued next page)

Box 6.3 (continued)

and (d) developing tools for analyzing tax policy, determining tax collection efficiency, and evaluating tax compliance.

Local revenue generation was realized by (a) a property spatial database kept up to date (with data provided through the central land agency and augmented by the local government); (b) a mass appraisal process consistent with the International Valuation Standard and based on real-market transactions; (c) a computerized tax collection system that integrates the property database, the valuation database, and the actual payments database; (d) a tax policy process that includes tax modeling, tax efficiency and compliance reporting, transparency, and engagement of stakeholders, including councils, businesses, and communities. A fifth key function, town planning and zoning, is also being implemented.

In the short term (12–18 months), implementation of the information systems yielded a 14–25 percent increase in local revenues (in the first six cities in the project). In the longer term (two years), a rigorous mass appraisal realized very large increases in the official schedule of market values of land: in Naga City, residential land values increased between 150 and 200 percent and commercial land values increased between 50 and 200 percent, while in Mandau City, where large investments in infrastructure had not been captured by updated market-based valuations for many years, the increases ranged from 300 to 2,300 percent in residential land values and from 1,500 to 2,900 percent in commercial land values. The greatly increased tax base and local ability to track future movements of the land market have allowed local governments to share the local tax burden more equitably and more transparently and to increase local revenues progressively.

Source: Land Equity International 2010.

The results from Ghana, the Philippines, and Thailand suggest that reforms in land tax policy and administration, especially ones that strengthen land records and property valuation, can lead to higher government revenue; this, in turn, is needed to improve decentralized governance and cost recovery in land administration. Experiences from these countries offer the following lessons for African countries aspiring to undertake reforms in land tax policy and administration:

- While driven by local governments, successful reforms require partnerships of government at all levels.

- Local governments must have access to better land administration services and information.

- Optimum results require integration of essential elements of local revenue generation, including a sound tax policy, a market-based tax assessment system that uses updated property and valuation databases, and a computerized tax collection system that is integrated with property, valuation, and payments databases.

Armed with these lessons, African countries can undertake homegrown land tax policy and administrative reforms, guided by generic guidelines on land and property tax policy such as the one produced by United Nations Habitat (UN-Habitat, GLTN 2011) and good-practice publications in tax policy such as those published by the International Monetary Fund (Gupta and Tareq 2008).

Strengthening Land Use Planning and Regulations for Sustainable Development

Strengthening the legal recognition and documentation of property rights and enabling them to be fully exercised are important for enhancing private investment and production. However, the state is responsible for protecting the social or public interest when individuals' land use decisions are detrimental to the public interest, due to either irrational behavior or unintended consequences (negative externalities). State intervention is justified when the actions of individual land users negatively affect landscapes, biodiversity, historic sites, or cultural values (Deininger 2003). The standard modes of intervention are land use planning and restrictions (regulations), which are becoming increasingly important not only to ensure effective management of land use but also to provide infrastructure and public services, to improve the urban and rural environment, to prevent pollution, and to pursue sustainable development (Williamson et al. 2010).[6] In developing countries and Sub-Saharan Africa in particular, where customary land tenure is predominant, land use planning has also become important for (a) identifying and delineating enough land for local individuals and communities as well as surplus land for use by entities outside the community, especially investors, and (b) delineating and facilitating improved group management of communally owned, pastoral, or protected lands, especially those covering large areas. Socially desirable government interventions for land use planning and restrictions require adequate "implementation capacity, transparent and fair allocation of costs and benefits, and predictable rules designed to minimize compliance costs" (Deininger 2003).

There are varying opinions on how land use planning and restrictions should be exercised. At one extreme, free market advocates, primarily in the United States, argue that landowners should be left alone to do what they want with their land; at the other extreme, central planning advocates, especially in Western Europe, subscribe to the principle that landowners should only do what is expressly allowed (a positive list), while everything else is forbidden. Laws in African and Asian countries previously colonized by Europe tend to reflect the central planning principle, although implementation and compliance are very weak (Williamson et al. 2010). The crux of the matter is how to balance land-owners' rights with the necessity and capacity of government to regulate land use in the best interests of society, a balance that can only be formalized in a national land policy developed with broad and deep consultations and implemented in a highly participatory manner (Williamson et al. 2010).

Land use planning processes in Ghana and Tanzania strike a reasonable balance between protecting private property rights and the public interest, while also promoting sustainable development by underpinning the planning process with national land policies adopted after broad consultations. Approval of land use plans by democratically elected authorities (in addition to technical authorities) and community participation in local or village land use plans and regularization schemes reinforce this balance of interests (see box 6.4). Ghana's and Tanzania's land use planning experiences offer two key lessons:

- Land use planning should be preceded and guided by national land policies.
- Local land use planning processes should be participatory and approved by democratically elected authorities.

These lessons should serve well African countries that are embarking on land use planning. Each country would be expected to develop planning guidelines that are best suited to its conditions. These can be drawn from generic planning guidelines such as those developed by United Nations Habitat (UN-Habitat, GLTN 2010).

BOX 6.4

Attempts to Strike the Right Balance between Individual and Public Interests in Land Use Planning in Ghana and Tanzania

Ghana's 1999 national land policy went through two years of broad consultations. It aims to ensure access to land and tenure security, while curbing land encroachment and unapproved development schemes and promoting participatory land use management and planning within a decentralized planning system. Property rights provisions are anchored in a new Land Bill, while planning provisions are in a new Land Use and Planning Bill (both to be approved by Parliament in 2012).

Ghana's three-tier model implements the plan's planning provisions using spatial development frameworks, structural plans, and local plans. Prepared at national, regional, subregional, and district levels, spatial development frameworks indicate present and future major land uses and transportation networks, boundaries of areas of special planning concern, and directions for further growth. They are not legal

(continued next page)

Box 6.4 (continued)

documents, but they must be approved by the appropriate authorities. Structural plans cover urban areas and their peripheries, showing present and proposed future development, including major land uses, roads, waterways, and railway lines, and areas of special planning concern or interest. They are legal planning documents, and they must be approved by the appropriate authorities. Local plans identify detailed land uses at the parcel level, with strong community participation. They must be approved by local authorities and form the basis for issuing planning and building permits.

Ghana's model has been successfully piloted in six districts and five regions. With support from the World Bank (World Bank 2011c) and private investment companies involved in oil exploration and development, planning guidelines and manuals have been prepared, information systems for planning land use have been developed, and capacity has been built to scale up to the whole country.

Tanzania's 1995 national land policy took five years of preparation and broad consultations; it both awards and protects land rights and restricts them to protect the public interest and promote sustainable development. Land use planning is anchored in the Land Use Planning Act 2007 and the Urban Planning Act 2007, themselves informed by the national environmental policy (1997), national forest policy (1998), national wildlife policy (1998), national human settlement policy (2000), national population policy (2002), and national livestock policy (2005). Provisions for land rights are anchored in the Land Act 1999 and the Village Land Act 1999. The Urban Planning Act 2007 regulates the preparation of general, detailed, and regularization schemes in urban areas, while the Land Use Planning Act 2007 regulates the planning in rural areas. The latter entails preparation of a national land use framework plan that guides (a) zonal and district land use plans and (b) land use for areas of national concern. District land use plans guide the preparation of village land use plans by the village community with the support of district land use officers. A 20-year national land use framework plan (2009–29) was prepared in 2010, and zonal and district land use framework plans have been prepared for a few priority areas. As of 2011, about 10 percent of Tanzania's nearly 12,000 villages had land use plans. National land use framework plans are not legal documents, but they must be approved by the authorities; village land use plans are legal documents, and they, too, must be approved by the authorities.

Source: Adapted from World Bank 2003, 2005c, 2011c.

Reforming Institutions and Developing Capacity for Land Administration

Developing capacity in land administration has to be approached at three levels: (a) at the societal level, addressing policy, institutions, systems, and the legal

Maps of Existing and Proposed Land Use in Matale Village, Bariadi District, Tanzania

a. Existing land use

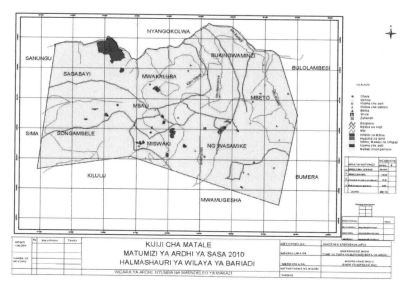

b. Proposed land use

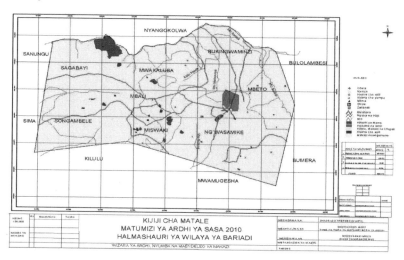

Credit: ©Chris Mnyanga, land component coordinator, Private Sector Competitiveness Project, Tanzania.

and regulatory framework; (b) at the organizational level, addressing culture, organization, management, resources, and procedures; and (c) at the individual level, addressing issues such as professional competence, education, and training (Williamson et al. 2010). In the context of Sub-Saharan Africa, it often involves undertaking institutional reforms and addressing shortages of skilled personnel.

Institutional Reform

Many institutions for land administration and management are fragmented and poorly coordinated in African countries. For example, in Ethiopia rural and urban lands are administered by different federal and regional government entities, with little coordination among them. While studies have been undertaken to address the issue of institutional fragmentation, institutional reforms have not yet been undertaken (World Bank 2011b). Ghana also has had severe problems of institutional fragmentation, although, unlike Ethiopia, bold institutional reforms have been undertaken, resulting in institutional mergers toward a single land agency. A National Lands Commission was established in 2008, bringing under one agency five key functions that were previously administered under separate agencies: deeds registration under the Lands Commission, land surveying under the Survey Department, title registration under the Land Title Registry, land valuation under the Land Valuation Board, and management of public and vested lands under the Lands Commission (World Bank 2011d). While a new building to enable the physical merger has not been completed, the operations are now managed by the National Lands Commission, which is autonomous from the oversight agency, the Ministry of Lands and Natural Resources. Although an independent evaluation of the impact of the merger has not yet been undertaken, early indications are that some improvements are being realized, especially in the sharing of information. In addition, the institutional reforms have improved efficiency in the delivery of services, with the time to transfer property declining from 169 days in 2005 to 34 days in 2011 (World Bank 2011c). The Ghana case suggests that reducing institutional fragmentation through mergers improves efficiency in land administration and management.

Addressing Shortages of Skilled Personnel

There is currently a scarcity of skilled land sector professionals across Sub-Saharan Africa. While Asian countries such as Malaysia and Sri Lanka have about 197 and 135 registered land surveyors per 1 million population, respectively, the bulk of African countries have less than a fourth of that; South Africa (among the most advanced) has only 31 surveyors, while Ghana, Tanzania, and Uganda each have fewer than 10 (see table 6.2).

The scarcity of personnel in Sub-Saharan Africa is not due to a lack of educational institutions or graduates. In fact, the colonial governments left behind

Table 6.2   Number of Professional Surveyors per Million Population in Select Countries

Region and country	Number of full-time-equivalent professional land surveyors per million population
Asia and Latin America	
Malaysia	196.6
Sri Lanka	135.0
Nepal	51.3
Mexico	41.0
Sub-Saharan Africa	
South Africa	31.3
Namibia	20.0
Ghana	6.3
Tanzania	3.8
Uganda	1.5

Source: Adapted from Williamson et al. 2010, except Ghana (from Ghana Institution of Surveyors), Uganda (from Surveyors Registration Board), and Tanzania (from National Council for Professional Surveyors).

educational institutions to train land specialists, especially land surveyors, as effective colonization required drawing administrative boundaries and demarcating land for colonial public institutions and white settlers. Land professionals were well trained, with professional associations (such as the institutions of surveyors and valuers) that are still in existence today. But with only a small fraction of land registered (10 percent of occupied land), formal land administration systems were small, and the land institutions became quickly saturated. Many land professionals became redundant or sought employment outside the land sector, especially in the building and construction industries. As of May 2012, only 85 of Kenya's 206 registered and licensed land surveyors were practicing in the country. With limited demand for professional graduates in the land sector, enrollment in the related educational institutions declined, and these institutions shifted to other areas of training or closed altogether (see box 6.5 for the experience of Ghana and Uganda).

In the last 10 years, there has been a revival and modernization of educational and training institutions and programs in response to renewed interest in land management and administration by African countries and their development partners. For example, in Ghana and Uganda, donor-funded projects have supported a variety of training, including on-the-job and in-college, for graduate professionals at different levels in the administration and management of land in public and private institutions. While such project-driven

BOX 6.5

Donor-Funded Land Administration Education and Training in Ghana and Uganda

Kwame Nkrumah University of Science and Technology (KNUST), which hosts the Center of Land Administration, was historically Ghana's main institute for professional education in surveying, mapping, land administration, and management, but by the early 2000s, it did not have adequate capacity to deliver high-caliber training in those fields. To strengthen research on land issues and training of technicians and specialists in land administration and management, the World Bank (2003) co-financed a project to purchase vehicles and modern digital surveying and mapping equipment for KNUST and for Kumasi Polytechnic University. Funding was also provided for establishing a global information system laboratory at KNUST and for conducting a collaborative study on divesting lands in Ghana's three northern regions. Furthermore, these institutions received textbooks and benefited from international seminars funded by the project.

Political instability in Uganda in the 1970s and 1980s led to an acute shortage of trained manpower for land management. Until 1997, the ministry responsible for land operated two separate postsecondary institutes dedicated to training technicians: the Survey School, which offered diplomas in land surveying, cartography, and land valuation, and the School of Physical Planning, which offered a diploma in physical planning. Both institutes closed in 1997, contributing substantially to the scarcity of technicians in the land sector. To address the shortage, a 2004 World Bank–funded project supported revival and modernization of the Survey School to train technicians for the land sector. Project funding also included construction of a resource center, including an administration block, a library, a computer lab, and lecture rooms; development of a strategy and business plan; basic furniture and instructional equipment (total stations and handheld global positioning units); and training of trainers conducted by international and local experts. Concurrently in 2005, the ministries responsible for land and education merged the two institutions into the School of Surveying and Land Management, which was renamed the Institute of Surveying and Land Management (ISLM) and resumed training. The ISLM, which opened in 2006 after rehabilitating the infrastructure of the former survey school, recruiting lecturers, and revamping the curriculum, offers diploma courses in land surveying, land management, land valuation, cartography, physical planning, and geo-informatics. The pioneer class graduated in 2008; these graduates and subsequent ones have been rapidly employed. The project also supported valuable short- and long-term training in local and regional institutions. Overseas training included three master's degrees in geodesy, valuation, and development economics and two diplomas in GIS and cartography.

Source: World Bank 2003, 2004b.

training is no doubt reducing the gap in skills, education and training need to be more comprehensive and cast in a longer-term framework that includes public sector reforms to attract and retain skilled professionals. Malawi made a good attempt at it in 2002. As it was finalizing a new land policy in the early 2000s, it faced a major constraint in capacity: in 2002, the country had only 26 qualified physical planners, 20 land valuation professionals, 12 licensed surveyors, and an identified deficit in the land sector of 400 professional staff and 800 technicians (Enemark and Ahene 2002). In response to this need, it developed three education or training programs: (a) a one-year certificate in land administration for land clerks, (b) a two-year diploma in surveying and land administration, and (c) a four-year bachelor's degree in surveying and land administration.

In-college training has to produce professionals able to meet today's demands, which are driven by new technology and new requirements. While land surveyors and valuers have traditionally dominated the field, more sociologists, anthropologists, information and communications technology specialists, land economists, and GIS experts are needed. Technical education in surveying and engineering has to be combined with management training in new technologies and the social and environmental elements of modern society, and in-college or vocational training has to be complemented with continuing professional training (Williamson et al. 2010). African governments and their development partners will have to respond by taking a comprehensive approach to education and training within a framework of at least 10 years.

Notes

1. They include Benin, Botswana, Burkina Faso, Ghana, Kenya, Madagascar, Malawi, Mali, Mauritius, Namibia, Nigeria, Rwanda, Senegal, Tanzania, Uganda, and Zambia.
2. Karnataka, Gujarat, Madhya Pradesh, Maharashtra, Rajasthan, and Tamil Nadu.
3. http://geoinfo.uneca.org/sdiafrica/default1.htm.
4. This section draws generously from Bruce (2012).
5. The transaction-based taxes include a registration fee, a stamp duty, a capital gains tax, and a speculation surcharge on transfers of land held for a short period. The bulk of the revenue is transmitted to the central treasury. While a building and land tax is collected by local governments, the tax and its administration are so weak that the revenue generated makes up less than 10 percent of total local government revenue (Amornvivat 2004).
6. A more market-oriented alternative to land use planning in handling negative externalities is to pay for environmental services, especially when the externality is harming a clearly identifiable group.

References

Ali, D., K. Deininger, and M. Goldstein. 2011. "Environmental and Gender Impacts of Land Tenure Regularization in Africa: Pilot Evidence from Rwanda." Policy Research Working Paper 5765, World Bank, Washington, DC.

Amornvivat, S. 2004. "Fiscal Decentralization: The Case of Thailand." Working Paper, Ministry of Finance, Thailand.

Bird, R. M., and E. Slack. 2004. *International Handbook on Land and Property Taxation.* Cheltenham, U.K.: Edward Edgar.

Brits, A. M., C. Grant, and T. Burns. 2002. "Comparative Study of Land Administration Systems with Special Reference to Thailand, Indonesia, and Karnataka (India)." Paper presented at the Regional Land Workshop, World Bank, Phnom Penh, June 4–6.

Bruce, J. 2012. "Decentralization of Land Administration: Recent African Experiences and Lessons Learned." Working Paper for the "Land Administration and Reforms in SSA" study, World Bank, Washington, DC.

Bruce, J. W., and A. Knox. 2009. "Structures and Stratagems: Decentralization of Authority over Land in Africa." *World Development* (special issue on the limits of state-led land reform) 37 (8): 1360–69.

Brueckner, J. K. 2000. "Fiscal Decentralization in Developing Countries: The Effects of Local Corruption and Tax Evasion." *Annals of Economics and Finance* 1 (1): 1–18.

Cheremshynskyi, M. 2012. "Development of Land Information Systems in Ghana and Uganda." Working Paper for the "Land Administration and Reform in SSA" study, World Bank, Washington, DC.

Deininger, K. 2003. *Land Policies for Growth and Poverty Reduction.* World Bank Policy Research Report. Washington, DC: World Bank; New York: Oxford University Press.

Deininger, K. 2008. "A Strategy for Improving Land Administration in India." Land Policy and Administration Notes 33, Agriculture and Rural Development, World Bank, Washington, DC, February.

Deininger, K., D. A. Ali, and T. Alemu. 2011. "Productivity Effects of Land Rental Markets in Ethiopia: Evidence from a Matched Tenant-Landlord Sample." Policy Research Working Paper 5727, World Bank, Washington, DC.

Deininger, K., and G. Feder. 2009. "Land Registration, Governance, and Development: Evidence and Implications for Policy." *World Bank Research Observer* 24 (2): 233–66.

Deininger, K., and A. Goyal. 2012. "Going Digital: Credit Effects of Land Registry Computerization in India." *Journal of Development Economics* 99 (2, November): 236–43. doi:10.1016/j.jdeveco.2012.02.007.

Enemark, S., and R. Ahene. 2002. "Capacity Building in Land Management: Implementing Land Policy Reforms in Malawi." Paper presented in session TS7.7, Twenty-Second International Congress, International Federation of Surveyors, Washington, DC, April 19–26.

GIC (Geo-Information Communication)/ESRI Canada. 2011. "Spatial Data Infrastructure for Monitoring Development Outcomes in Uganda." InfoDev/World Bank, Washington, DC.

Gupta, T., and S. Tareq. 2008. "Mobilizing Revenue: Strengthening Domestic Revenue Bases Is Key to Creating Fiscal Space for Africa's Developmental Needs." *Finance and Development* 45 (3, September): n.p.

Land Equity International. 2010. "Philippines Land Administration and Management Project (LAMP2), Activity Completion Report on AusAID–World Bank–funded LAMP2 Project." AusAID, Canberra, Australia.

Lunnay, C. 2005. "Land Administration in the Asian Region: Challenges and Opportunities." Presented at the Expert Group Meeting, "Secure Land: New Legal Frameworks and Tools," United Nations Economic and Social Commission for Asia and the Pacific, Bangkok, December 8–9.

McLaren, R. A. 2011. "Module 12: ICT for Land Administration [and Natural Resource Management]." Draft version 1.0–27/4/2011, working Document, World Bank, Washington, DC.

Murage, E. M., P. Gitimu, and J. Sato. 2008. "The Project of Strengthening of Survey of Kenya for GIS Promotion in the Republic of Kenya." *International Archives of the Photogrammetry, Remote Sensing, and Spatial Information Sciences* 37 (pt. B6a): 117–22. Beijing.

Nolte, K. 2012. "Large-Scale Agricultural Investments under Poor Land Governance Systems: Actors and Institutions in the Case of Zambia." Paper presented at the Annual Conference "Land and Poverty," World Bank, Washington, DC, April 23–26.

Oloo, J. O. 2011. "Assessing the Development of the Kenya National Spatial Data Infrastructure." MSc thesis, Wageningen University, Wageningen, Norway.

Ribot, J. C. 2001. "Local Actors, Powers, and Accountability in African Decentralization: A Review of Key Issues." Paper prepared for the IDRC, Canada, Assessment of Social Policy Reforms Initiative, World Resources Institute, Washington, DC.

Sikor, T., and D. Muller. 2009. "The Limits of State-Led Land Reform: An Introduction." *World Development* (special issue on the limits of state-led land reform) 37 (8): 1307–16.

UN-Habitat (United Nations Habitat), GLTN (Global Land Tool Network). 2010. *Citywide Strategic Planning: A Guideline*. Nairobi: United Nations Print Shop. http://www.gltn.net/en/home/land-use-planning/citywide-strategic-planning-guidelines/details.html.

———. 2011. "Land and Property Tax: A Policy Guide." United Nations Habitat, GLTN, Nairobi, October 8. http://www.gltn.net/en/home/land-tax-and-valuation/land-and-property-tax-a-policy-guide/download.html.

Williamson, I., S. Enemark, J. Wallace, and A. Rajabffard. 2010. *Land Administration for Sustainable Development*. Redlands, CA: ESRI Press Academic.

World Bank. 2003. "Ghana Land Administration Project." Project Appraisal Document, World Bank, Washington, DC.

———. 2004a. "Malawi Community-Based Rural Land Development Project." Project Appraisal Document, World Bank, Washington, DC.

———. 2004b. "Uganda Second Private Sector Competitiveness Project." Project Appraisal Document, World Bank, Washington, DC.

———. 2005a. "Philippines Second Land Administration and Management Project." World Bank, Washington, DC.

————. 2005b. "Tanzania Private Sector Competitiveness Project." Project Appraisal Document, World Bank, Washington, DC.

————. 2005c. "Uganda Second Private Sector Competitiveness Project, Land Component Project Implementation Manual." World Bank, Washington, DC.

————. 2007. "India: Land Policies for Growth and Poverty Reduction." World Bank, Washington, DC.

————. 2011a. *Doing Business 2012: Doing Business in a More Transparent World.* Washington, DC: World Bank.

————. 2011b. "Ethiopia: Options for Strengthening Land Administration in Ethiopia." World Bank, Washington, DC.

————. 2011c. "Ghana Land Administration Project." Implementation Completion and Results Report, World Bank, Washington, DC.

————. 2011d. "Ghana Second Land Administration Project." Project Appraisal Document, World Bank, Washington, DC.

————. 2011e. "Madagascar Land Administration and Management Technical Assistance." World Bank, Washington, DC.

————. 2011f. "Policy Note on Rural Land Taxation in Mozambique." World Bank, Washington, DC.

Chapter 7

Implications for Scaling Up Land Administration and Reforms

Scaling up land administration and reforms in Sub-Saharan Africa has several dimensions. First, it is important to clarify the role of key players, primarily pan-African organizations, African governments, the private sector, civil society, and development partners. Second, it is necessary to clarify exactly what is to be scaled up, the pathways to scaling up, and the costs and benefits of the effort. This chapter elaborates on these dimensions of scaling up, starting with the role of key players, as outlined in table 7.1.

The Role of Pan-African Organizations

To scale up comprehensive policy reforms and investments, African governments will have to act collectively at the regional level and individually at the country level. At the regional level, the Land Policy Initiative (LPI) is the key institution created to spearhead the implementation of a rigorous roadmap. The LPI facilitated regional assessments and consultative workshops across Africa, which culminated in the development and endorsement of the *Framework and Guidelines on Land Policy in Africa* by African Union (AU) ministers responsible for land and agriculture in April 2009. The framework was endorsed at the highest level of Africa's governance by the AU Heads of State and Government summit in July 2009, through the *AU Declaration on Land Issues and Challenges* (box 7.1).

In its second phase, the LPI aims to assist African countries with implementation of the declaration, in accordance with the framework and guidelines, and to facilitate equitable access to land and tenure security for land users in both customary and statutory jurisdictions. Specifically, the LPI is expected to undertake the following:

- Highlight and advocate for the recognition of land in the development agenda of African member states
- Galvanize efforts and partnerships in support of land policy development and implementation

163

Table 7.1 Scaling Up Land Administration: The Role of Key Players in Sub-Saharan Africa

Key element	Role of key players				
	Pan-African organizations	African governments	Development partners	Private sector	Civil society
Policy reforms	Advocates; coordinators; monitors and evaluators	Policy makers	Advisers; coordinators	Advocates	Advocates
Investment	Resource mobilizers; monitors and evaluators	Resource mobilizers and investors; implementers	Resource mobilizers; donors and creditors; coordinators; knowledge transferors	Investors and creditors; contractors; technology brokers	Monitors and evaluators

- Facilitate policy dialogue, capacity development, and resource mobilization for member states
- Promote professional networking and knowledge sharing
- Develop and build capacity for monitoring and evaluation tools and systems
- Provide technical support and advisory services to regional economic communities and member states on developing and implementing land policy (African Union, UN Economic Commission for Africa, and African Development Bank n.d.).

The role envisaged for the LPI is laudable; the challenge is in implementation, especially since the LPI is a young institution currently in the process of building itself while also gearing up to meet its mandate. The LPI's establishment is timely for scaling up land administration and reform in Sub-Saharan Africa and the rest of Africa, and its 5-year strategic plan coincides with the first 5-year phase of the 10-year scaling-up program advocated in this report. It would be appropriate for global and regional organizations working on land issues in Africa to build synergies with and support the efforts of the LPI, to augment its strategic plan, and to contribute to its ultimate success.

The Role of African Governments

At the country level, African governments are expected to undertake at least four actions to scale up their land administration programs:

- Prepare or update their national land policies, as Rwanda did in 2004 and Kenya in 2009 (Ali, Deininger, and Goldstein 2011; United Republic of Kenya 2009).

BOX 7.1
_____

The *AU Declaration on Land Issues and Challenges*: Commitments and Responsibilities

In the declaration on land, the AU Heads of State and Government committed to the following:

- Initiate the development, implementation, and monitoring of comprehensive land policy in an inclusive manner, involving civil society organizations, the private sector, and other concerned stakeholders
- Allocate adequate budgetary resources for such land policy processes
- Ensure that land laws provide all users of land with equitable access to land and land-related resources, giving special attention to strengthening the land rights of African women.

The declaration called on member states to take note of the principles and steps outlined by the framework and urged them to do the following:

- Review their land sectors with a view to developing comprehensive policies that take into account their particular needs
- Build adequate human, technical, and financial capacity in support of land policy development, implementation, and monitoring.

The declaration invited regional economic communities to do the following:

- Convene periodic regional platforms to facilitate experience sharing, lesson learning, and dissemination of best practices in the formulation and implementation of land policy
- Appropriately capture and address land policy issues within a common agricultural policy framework.

The Heads of State and Government also requested the consortium on land policy of the African Union Commission, the United Nations Economic Commission for Africa, and the African Development Bank to do the following:

- Establish an appropriate institutional framework (including a fund) to coordinate and support implementation activities of the declaration
- Take appropriate actions to establish a mechanism for tracking of progress and for periodic reporting by member states.

Source: African Union 2009.

_____

- Prepare long-term land sector strategic plans or programs in a fashion similar to Thailand's successful 20-year Land Titling Program (Brits, Grant, and Burns 2002), as Tanzania and Uganda did in the 10-year strategic plan for implementation of the land laws and the 10-year land sector strategic plan, respectively (United Republic of Tanzania 2005; Government of Uganda 2001). Experience from Thailand suggests that these long-term plans play an important role in nurturing long-term political and donor commitment to supporting the land sector, providing a framework for investing in land administration by the public sector, and signaling to private sector professionals the pace at which they should build capacity to service the land sector (Brits, Grant, and Burns 2002).

- Mobilize domestic and foreign funding to prepare and implement 10-year programs in two 5-year phases, using each phase to align and harmonize assistance from development partners, while keeping the program from fragmenting into uncoordinated projects.

- Allocate greater funding for the land sector from the national budget. The land sector has been grossly underfunded in Sub-Saharan Africa, suffering the same fate as agriculture, which received less than 4 percent of total public spending in 2004 compared to 10 percent in 1980. The New Partnership for Africa's Development advocates that the share of public expenditure on agriculture should be 10 percent (World Bank 2007). Gross underfunding of the land sector by African countries is evidenced in Tanzania, which, in the last eight years, allocated less than 20 percent of the required funding from the national budget to implement national land policies and laws (see box 7.2). Across Sub-Saharan Africa, budget allocations have been so low that national land sector budgets will have to increase by a factor of two to three to make any significant progress. But African governments do not have to wait for donor support. The Ethiopian and Rwandan governments have successfully supported their land sectors, with donor assistance playing only a supplemental or no role at all (see box 7.3). Fortunately, scaling up public investments in the land sector is bound to generate greater returns now than in the past, given the surge in commodity prices since 2008 and major recent increases in foreign direct investment, which have the potential to increase agricultural yields and markets (Deininger, Ali, and Alemu 2011).

The Role of the Private Sector and Civil Society

The private sector can support scaling-up efforts by investing in land administration, for example, by developing computerized land information systems (LISs) and continuously operating reference stations (CORSs) using investment models, including build, own, operate, and transfer, with revenue coming from

BOX 7.2

Problems with Tanzania's Land Sector Budget

In fiscal 2012 (July 1, 2011, to June 30, 2012), Tanzania's Ministry of Lands, Housing, and Human Settlement Development received a budget allocation of TSh 16.22 billion, equivalent to about US$10 million, out of a national budget of TSh 9.62 trillion (US$6.4 billion), representing 0.17 percent of the budget. As of May 2012, only TSh 1.86 billion had been released, less than 12 percent of the allocated funds. While it might be premature to draw a conclusion based on one year of budget data, Tanzania's 10-year strategic plan for implementation of the land laws (2005–06 to 2014–15) was equally underbudgeted and underspent. As of May 2012, only two and a half years before the end of the plan, less than US$50 million out of the planned US$300 million had been spent (about 17 percent). This underfunding occurred despite the existence of a national land policy backed by laws deemed to provide an adequate basis for sound land administration (Alden Wily 2003) and despite the facts that land disputes are clogging the courts and less than 5 percent of rural land is registered.

Source: Based on data collected from the Ministry of Lands, Housing, and Human Settlement Development.

service charges over the period of the contract. A project in the Philippines demonstrated that this usually takes about 10 years (Warnest and Bell 2009). The private sector can also support scaling-up efforts by contracting to supply civil works, goods, and services. An important role for civil society is advocating for good policies and practices, as well as acting as an independent monitor and evaluator of the processes for designing and implementing policies. For example, the Kenya Land Alliance played an important advocacy and monitoring role in the design and implementation of Kenya's national land policy, approved by Parliament in 2009; key land policy principles were reflected in Kenya's new constitution, enacted in 2010 (USAID 2009–10). Associations of land professionals such as surveyors and valuers should continue to play their traditional role of upholding quality standards and advocating for good policies and practices. They should also play a role in training and mentoring their members to meet the higher demand for services expected as a result of the scale-up of land administration in Sub-Saharan Africa.

The Role of Development Partners

African governments need not act alone. Their efforts can and should be complemented with support from development partners to shorten the reform process and to enrich the quality of implementation of land policy and

BOX 7.3

Government Commitment: Key to Success in Ethiopia and Rwanda

During 2003–05, Ethiopia delineated and adjudicated 20 million land parcels and issued about 5 million land certificates in three of its main regions (Amhara, Oromia, and Southern Nations Nationalities, Peoples' Region [SNNPR]), a pace matched only by Vietnam in the 1990s after it abandoned collective farming. Ethiopia's registration methodology did not survey or map land boundaries, but it provided enough security of tenure to have a significant impact on investment and gender equity (Deininger et al. 2007). Moreover, its land registration program was undertaken without support from development partners; support came only after completion of the program and went for piloting various approaches to mapping boundaries in the second stage of registration. While not all is well in Ethiopia's land policy, especially given restrictions on renting, selling, and mortgaging rural land, Ethiopian authorities clearly are committed to improving land administration and management, with or without support from development partners.

After adopting a national land policy in June 2004 and passing an Organic Land Law in 2005, the government of Rwanda piloted systematic land registration during 2007 and 2008. It then embarked on a five-year plan to scale up its land registration program to the whole country from 2009 to 2013. In contrast to Ethiopia, Rwanda's registration program is already well established, with a process for marking boundaries on an orthophoto map, computerizing information collected from the field, and providing landholders with the rights to rent, sell, and mortgage rural land. The program was completed in June 2012, well ahead of schedule. An impact evaluation study found that the program is having a significant impact on investment and gender equity (Ali, Deininger, and Goldstein 2011). While development partners led by the U.K. Department for International Development have provided funding in the range of US$40 million, the success of the program in terms of speed, coverage, and impact is clearly due to the government's commitment to improve land administration and avoid land conflicts, which have contributed to civil war in the past.

---

administration programs by sharing global experiences, providing financial resources, and supporting monitoring and evaluation systems to track performance at the country level. Donor support for the land sector in Sub-Saharan Africa has been grossly inadequate, similar to that for agriculture, whose share in official development assistance declined from a high of 18 percent in 1979 to 3.5 percent in 2004 (World Bank 2007). For example, as of June 2012, the World Bank's total commitments to ongoing projects or components of projects supporting land activities were US$226 million. While these commitments were nine times higher than the US$25.4 million total commitments in 2001, they were equivalent to only 0.5 percent of the US$41.2 billion total commitments to Sub-Saharan Africa by the World Bank (and the International Development Agency) as of June 4, 2012. The commitments supported only one stand-alone project, the Ghana Land Administration Project, Phase Two (US$50 million), while the rest of the funding went to support land components scattered in 21 projects belonging to other sectors. In addition to being inadequately funded by all measures, the land activities supported were overshadowed by the projects under which they were funded and therefore received limited attention from African governments and the World Bank itself. There is no evidence to indicate that other development partners provided adequate funding for land or delivered it more effectively; on the contrary, indications are that they provided even less funding than the World Bank. To rectify the situation, development partners not only should significantly scale up funding, but also should channel it through programs, which are more effective in addressing sector priorities, rather than through projects.

Development partners can increase the effectiveness of their funding by improving coordination at the global level by hosting annual consultations and conferences and at the country level by harmonizing and aligning the delivery of aid. Funding should be timely, consistent, adequate, and committed to long-term programs of at least 10 years to assure governments that the commitment is long lasting. The missed opportunities from going slowly or providing inadequate support to land policies and administration are high in terms of forgone investments, jobs, and growth from land-based resources that could otherwise boost African and global economies. Not acting fast enough could contribute to frustration, reversal of land policy reforms, and economic decline, as happened with Zimbabwe's land reform in the late 1990s and 2000s (see box 7.4).

Development partners can also help by supporting analytical work to prioritize and evaluate interventions. For example, the land governance assessment framework (LGAF), developed by the World Bank in partnership with some multilateral and bilateral partners and with other development stakeholders, including some pan-African institutions, can be used to assess the status of land governance at the country level in a participatory process, to establish a consensus on priority actions, and to pilot and track progress in their implementation (see box 7.5).

Dimensions of Scaling Up: What, How, and at What Cost?

The scaling-up effort involves at least 10 key elements, with many African countries involved in one or more of them. It is estimated to cost about US$4.5 billion over a 10-year period (table 7.2).

The first element for scaling up is "improving tenure security over communal lands," estimated to cost about US$0.40 billion. This will typically involve

BOX 7.4

Lack of Donor Funding for Land Reform in Zimbabwe, 1979–2009

Land reform in Zimbabwe originated in the 1979 signing of the Lancaster House Agreement, which paved the way for independence. The agreement included provisions to distribute land more equitably between historically disenfranchised black Africans and the minority white Africans who ruled Zimbabwe from 1890 to 1979. The government's land distribution strategy can be divided into two periods: from 1979 to 2000, the "willing-seller willing-buyer" (WSWB) approach was applied, with economic assistance largely from Great Britain; in 2000, this was replaced by a fast-track land reform program, characterized by an often violent takeover of white-owned farmlands without compensation. The latter set in motion Zimbabwe's current state of political instability and economic stagnation, with high levels of poverty.

Donors had two windows of opportunity to change the direction of land reform in Zimbabwe. The first opportunity came at a donor conference in 1981 called by the government of Zimbabwe; only the British government put money on the table to purchase land for the reform program. The second opportunity was at a donor conference in 1998, where donors endorsed the program (a combined market and state acquisition of land), but neither they nor the government of Zimbabwe followed through with funding and implementation. Had the donor community acted decisively and committed funding at the 1981 and 1998 conferences, Zimbabwe might not have descended into economic collapse and political instability.

Source: Adapted from Rukuni, Nyoni, and Sithole 2009; World Bank 2004.

(a) organizing and formalizing communal groups and (b) demarcating boundaries and registering the rights of the formalized groups. This element of scaling up is particularly urgent in countries with large chunks of communal land, such as Angola, the Democratic Republic of Congo, Mozambique, Tanzania, and Zambia. Until recently, registration of communal land was not urgent, because the rights of community members in many countries were quite secure and demand for land from noncommunity members was minimal. However, as investors have become more interested in land for large-scale farming, communal lands have become targets for investors. It has therefore become necessary to establish or strengthen institutions to register and manage communal lands, as Ghana, Mozambique, and Tanzania have done. Once communal land is registered, individual holdings within communities can be registered over time, as these are less vulnerable to claims from outside. Moreover, land claims and disputes within communities are easier to handle after communal land has been registered due to clearer rules of land administration. The total cost of registering all communal

BOX 7.5

The Land Governance Assessment Framework

Developed by the World Bank in partnership with the Food and Agriculture Organization (FAO), United Nations Habitat (UN-Habitat), the International Fund for Agricultural Development (IFAD), the International Food Policy Research Institute (IFPRI), the African Union, and bilateral partners, the LGAF is a diagnostic tool for assessing the status of land governance at the country level in a participatory process of three to six months. Drawing systematically on local expertise and existing evidence rather than on outsiders, it focuses on five key areas—recognition and enforcement of rights; land use planning, land management, and taxation; management of public land; public provision of land information; and dispute resolution and conflict management—with optional modules for other topics (large-scale acquisition of land and forests) that have traditionally often been dealt with in isolation from each other. This process helps to establish a consensus and priority actions on (a) gaps in existing evidence; (b) areas for regulatory or institutional change, piloting of new approaches, and interventions to improve land governance on a broader scale; and (c) criteria to assess the effectiveness of these measures. The LGAF helps to put in place a structure and process to track progress in improving land governance systematically over time.

The core LGAF process is guided by 21 land governance indicators in the 5 key areas listed above, each divided into 3–4 dimensions for which rankings are assigned by expert panels based on precoded answers on a scale from A to D. Implementation involves several discrete steps that are overseen by a country coordinator, a well-respected and impartial person with extensive knowledge of the sector. In a preparation phase, the team is set up and government buy-in is sought. Background documentation (using available information and data) is then prepared to facilitate assessment of the indicators. Expert panels are then convened to discuss the dimensions in detail to arrive at a consensus ranking and agree on policy priorities. A report is then written and presented at a national workshop, which validates the results and prioritizes policy conclusions and associated monitoring indicators. The report is presented to key policy makers at a subsequent policy workshop, preferably organized immediately thereafter.

Following initial pilots in Ethiopia, Indonesia, the Kyrgyz Republic, Peru, and Tanzania to demonstrate the viability of the analytical concept, a first round of assessments was completed in Benin, Georgia, Ghana, Madagascar, Malawi, Nigeria, South Africa, and Ukraine. Experience in these countries indicates that the exercise has the potential to increase the scope, quality, and acceptance of public policies by (a) improving communication among stakeholders within and outside the government to create a constituency for reform; (b) increasing awareness, coordination, and integrated monitoring of key land sector initiatives; and (c) feeding into broader country strategies by providing ministries of finance and development partners with a set of broadly backed and actionable recommendations that lend themselves to inclusion in development strategies and flexible instruments of project and budget support.

Source: Extracted from Deininger, Selod, and Burns 2012.

Table 7.2 Key Elements of and Pathways to Scaling Up Land Administration in Sub-Saharan Africa

Key element	Cost estimate (US$ billion)	Scaling-up pathways: Lessons learned and good practices
1. Improving tenure security over communal lands	0.40	• Organizing and formalizing communal groups • Demarcating boundaries and registering communal rights
2. Improving tenure security over individual lands	1.00	• Undertaking systematic titling with a spatial framework based on low-cost simple technology and without using a boundary survey for low-value rural land • Undertaking systematic titling based on a detailed survey of boundaries for urban and high-value rural land
3. Increasing land access and tenure for the poor and vulnerable	0.50	• Redistributing rural land using the willing-seller willing-buyer approach • Regularizing rights of squatters on urban public land • Removing restrictions on land rental markets • Promoting gender equity with favorable laws and documentation of rights
4. Increasing efficiency and transparency in land administration services	1.30	• Decentralizing the empowerment of local communities and traditional authorities, with clear provisions for social and financial sustainability • Computerizing and developing land information systems and national spatial data infrastructure • Modernizing surveying and mapping infrastructure, including geodetic referencing, base mapping, and cadastral systems
5. Developing capacity in land administration	0.40	• Undertaking institutional and policy reforms to guide capacity development • Undertaking training and knowledge transfer
6. Resolving land disputes and managing expropriations	0.20	• Resolving disputes by building competent institutions, including strengthening judicial institutions and removing backlogs, creating specialized tribunals, training judges, and empowering alternative forums and approaches • Managing expropriations, including updating laws, paying fair and full compensation, adhering to the principle of eminent domain, and improving the environment for governance

(continued next page)

Table 7.2 (continued)

7. Increasing scope and effectiveness of land use planning	0.40	• Ensuring that land use planning is guided by a national land policy
		• Undertaking spatial planning frameworks at national, regional, and district levels to guide local planning in urban and rural areas
		• Undertaking local land use planning in a participatory way and using plans approved by democratically elected authorities
8. Improving public land management	0.10	• Inventorying, surveying, and registering all public lands
		• Ensuring that land not critical for public goods and services is allocated to the poor in a transparent process or to investors in a competitive process
9. Developing postconflict land administration	0.10	• At the end of conflicts, focusing early on managing land-related conflicts and developing land policies to address the underlying tensions
		• Ensuring that development partners deploy technical assistance early and rapidly to advise on resolution of policy issues
		• Reestablishing technical capacity to rebuild land administration
		• Where governance institutions are weak or absent, using task forces and special commissions to fill the gap
10. Strengthening valuation functions and land tax policies	0.05	• While driven by local governments, developing partnerships of government at all levels
		• Providing local governments with access to better land administration services and information
		• Integrating essential elements of local revenue generation, including a sound tax policy, a tax assessment system, and a computerized tax collection system
Total	4.50[a]	

a. Amounts have been rounded up.

lands in a country can range from US$10 million to US$15 million if communities are already organized, as in Tanzania, or from US$25 million to US$30 million if communities are not yet organized.[1] Based on the experiences of Ghana, Mexico, Mozambique, and Tanzania, the scaling-up program's goal of having the key relevant countries register all of their community lands within 10 years is achievable.

The second element is "improving tenure security over individual lands," with an estimated cost of US$1.00 billion. In rural areas where land values are relatively low, tenure of individual rights will be secured through systematic titling using a spatial framework that relies on low-cost simple technology and "general-boundary" principles, while for urban and higher-value rural lands, tenure security will be achieved through systematic titling based on a detailed survey of boundaries. The target for scaling up systematic titling in rural areas is to register all prime rural lands, using a proxy of 50 percent of the arable lands in a country. Mauritius, Rwanda, and South Africa have already achieved this goal. Ethiopia and Kenya are close, at about 40 percent, while Tanzania has registered less than 5 percent of its estimated 25 million rural land parcels. Tanzania will need to invest about US$125 million just to register half of its rural lands, assuming that it reduces the registration cost per unit to that of Rwanda (US$10 per parcel) by using a photomap to capture land boundaries. Countries with high population densities and higher-value rural lands, requiring a detailed survey of land boundaries, will incur registration costs per unit at least double that (US$20 per parcel). For example, it will cost Ghana and Uganda both at least US$40 million to register their high-value lands (2 million land parcels each). With satellite and information and communications technologies continuing to reduce the costs of surveying and registering land and computerizing land records, the costs of administering communal and individual land rights will probably continue to fall. Thus African countries should continue piloting new approaches even as they embark on scaling up.

The third element for scaling up is "increasing land access and tenure for the poor and vulnerable," with an estimated cost of US$0.50 billion, through four pathways: (a) redistributing underused rural land using participatory, subsidized, and WSWB approaches, as in Kenya, Malawi, and South Africa; (b) regularizing the rights of squatters in urban slums on public land, as initiated in Kenya, Lesotho, and Tanzania; (c) removing restrictions on land rental markets, as initiated in Ethiopia; and (d) promoting gender equity with favorable laws and documentation of rights, as in Ethiopia and Rwanda. A successful redistribution of land in the countries with former colonial settlements would not only reduce land inequalities and landlessness but also raise the incomes of vulnerable segments of society; it also would provide workable models to address landownership inequalities in other countries in the region. This book estimates that about US$180 million would be required to build a strong foundation for land redistribution in six countries over 10 years, while about US$300 million would be required to scale up regularization of land tenure in urban slums in 30 countries over 10 years. Scaling up support for promoting gender equality and enhancing land rental markets will take considerable effort in the way of policy and legal reforms.

The fourth element for scaling up is "increasing efficiency and transparency in land administration services." This element involves the most countries (about 40) and will cost the most money (about 30 percent of the total cost).

The estimated cost is about US$1.30 billion. The element has three pathways to scaling up: (a) decentralization to empower local communities and traditional authorities, with clear provisions for social and financial sustainability; (b) computerization and development of land information systems and national spatial data infrastructure; and (c) modernization of surveying and mapping infrastructure, including geodetic referencing, base mapping, and cadastral systems. This scaling up will help to overhaul and modernize the infrastructure and systems of land administration inherited at independence. An easily measurable indicator of progress is the number of days to transfer property or land in a public land registry. One aim of scaling up should be to eliminate the efficiency gap between Sub-Saharan Africa (65 days) and Organisation for Economic Co-operation and Development countries (31 days) within 10 years. This goal is achievable: nine African countries had achieved it by December 2011 (World Bank 2011), and there is no reason why the rest of Sub-Saharan Africa could not do so within 10 years.[2]

The fifth element for scaling up is "developing capacity in land administration," with an estimated cost of US$0.40 billion, to be undertaken through institutional and policy reforms, training, and knowledge transfer. Done concurrently with the expansion of land administration services, capacity development would have a greater chance to succeed than in the past because there would be effective demand for and absorption of trained people within the land sector. In the past, trained land professionals such as registered surveyors encountered no effective demand for their services in the land sector and hence sought employment elsewhere, such as in the growing building and construction industry (see chapter 6).

The remaining five elements for scaling up would cost an estimated US$0.85 billion and include the following:

- Resolving land disputes and managing expropriations, as in Ghana, by building competent institutions to dispose of land cases speedily and effectively and by updating expropriations and compensation laws and paying full and fair compensation (estimated cost: US$0.20 billion). Progress would be measured in terms of ease of access to systems for resolving land disputes and the average speed and cost involved in resolving the cases.

- Increasing the coverage, effectiveness, and efficiency of land use planning, as in Ghana and Tanzania, guided by national land policies and using participatory principles for local planning (estimated cost: US$0.40 billion). Success would be tracked in terms of developing and implementing sustainable models of land use planning.

- Increasing efficiency and transparency in the management and use of public land, as in Ghana and Uganda, by taking land inventories and using competitive and transparent mechanisms to dispose of surplus public lands (estimated cost: US$0.10 billion).

- Developing postconflict land administration, as in Liberia and Rwanda, by focusing early on managing land-related conflicts and developing land policies and capacity to address the underlying tensions and rebuild land administration (estimated cost: US$0.10 billion). Progress would be measured in terms of reestablishing land administration.

- Developing land valuation functions and land tax policies by providing local governments with better land information and administration services and a combination of a sound land tax policy, a tax assessment system, and a computerized tax collection system (estimated cost: US$0.05 billion). Progress would be tracked in terms of additional revenue raised from land-related taxes and charges.

The cost estimates of scaling up are based on implementation experiences and case studies as well as on assessments of readiness of countries to engage in one or more elements of the scaling-up program. For registering communal land rights, cost estimates are based on covering 30 countries at nearly US$15 million each; for registering individual rights, coverage is 25 countries at US$40 million each; for providing land access for the poor and vulnerable, coverage includes US$60 million each for three countries for redistributing land, US$10 million each for 30 countries for regularizing tenure in urban slums, and US$20 million for promoting gender equity and freer rental markets for agricultural land across the region; for overhauling land administration services, coverage is 40 countries at about US$35 million each; for developing capacity, coverage is 27 countries at about US$15 million each; for resolving land disputes, coverage is 20 countries at about US$10 million each; for land use planning, coverage is 20 countries for US$20 million each; for public land management, coverage is 10 countries for US$10 million each; for postconflict land administration, coverage is 5 countries for US$20 million each; and for valuation and land tax policies, coverage is 10 countries for US$5 million each.

Country-Specific Opportunities for Scaling Up

Not every country will participate in every element of scaling up. The need and readiness to scale up are specific to each country. While many countries have the need to and can quickly prepare themselves to scale up investments to modernize infrastructure, develop capacity, and improve efficiency and transparency in land administration services, few are ready to scale up investments in low-cost approaches for registering communal and individual land rights. For the latter, some extensive piloting may be needed before scaling up. Other countries need to undertake analytical work and assessments to identify key land issues and actions and to prepare strategic plans for scaling up. While programs to scale up have to be prioritized and prepared using internal processes within each country, it is still possible to suggest areas of need for scaling up based on gross country characteristics:

- Countries with large communal areas typically targeted by foreign direct investment in large-scale agriculture have a need to scale up investments in land use planning and registration of communal lands; for example, Angola, the Democratic Republic of Congo, Ghana, Mozambique, Tanzania, and Zambia.

- Countries with high population density and more individualized landholdings are good candidates for scaling up investments in registration of individual land rights; for example, Ethiopia, Madagascar, Malawi, Rwanda, and Uganda.

- Postconflict countries need to invest in the development of land policies and capacity to address the underlying tensions and to rebuild land administration to avoid future conflicts; for example, Burundi, Côte d'Ivoire, Liberia, Sierra Leone, and South Sudan.

- Countries with large and growing numbers of urban squatters settled on government land are good candidates to scale up investments in regularizing the land rights of slum dwellers; for example, Angola, Ethiopia, Kenya, Mozambique, Tanzania, and Zambia.

- Countries with high levels of landownership inequality and landlessness can benefit from peaceful and equitable redistribution of land; for example, Kenya, Malawi, and South Africa.

- Virtually all African countries would benefit from and can prepare themselves quickly to scale up investments in developing land valuation functions and land tax policies and in improving public land management, resolving land disputes, and managing expropriations.

The implications of scaling up in Sub-Saharan Africa are not trivial. African governments and their development partners will need to invest massively in the land sector. Modalities of financing need to change from small projects and land components meant to support studies and pilots to land sector programs intended to cover a whole country over an extended period of at least 10 years. For example, Tanzania's collection of donor-funded small projects has totaled less than US$50 million over the past 10 years, but scaling up adequately requires a 10-year land sector program of at least US$200 million. Ghana has been implementing the second phase of its Land Administration Project (US$70 million), but scaling up there means accelerating the current project and following it with a sectorwide program to complete the remaining land policy development and administration agenda. These are just two examples illustrating the range, complexity, and cost of scaling up. Within the next two to three years, virtually all African countries and their development partners will need to complete their land sector assessments to identify key issues and actions and prepare strategic plans and medium-term programs and projects to guide the scale-up of investments in land administration. To accomplish even this requires mobilizing resources and financing the actual scale-up of investments in land administration.

Benefits of the Scaling-Up Program

The scaling-up program, which has 10 elements, produces benefits that fall under 5 categories: economic growth, poverty reduction, conflict prevention and management, environmental protection, and good governance.

Economic Growth

All 10 elements of the scaling-up program contribute either directly or indirectly to economic growth through several pathways that enhance investment or the productivity of investment, including (a) increased incentives for investment, especially from land tenure security; (b) an overall increase in productivity as land moves from less efficient to more efficient producers through rental and sales markets; (c) value added through land information; and (d) increased access to more and cheaper credit through use of land as collateral. Ample empirical evidence confirms that these contribute to economic growth, especially through the impacts of secure land tenure and efficient delivery of land on investment, described in chapter 2. For Sub-Saharan Africa in particular, the most recent evidence of a strong positive relationship between land tenure security and investment was found in impact studies that measured the relationship between documentation of land rights and investment in Ethiopia and Rwanda. On a higher level, strengthening land tenure security reduces the risk of dispossessing local communities and ensures investors' deals, both of which are critical to accelerating and sustaining growth in Africa.

Poverty Reduction

The goal of reducing poverty is targeted more directly by redistributing land to the landless, the poor, and the vulnerable; removing restrictions on rental markets for agricultural land; increasing women's access to land; and regularizing land tenure for squatters on public land in urban slums. The benefits of redistributing land to the land poor are demonstrated by the Malawi pilot project, whose beneficiaries increased their agricultural incomes by 40 percent per year (see chapter 3), while evidence from China and Vietnam confirms large impacts of rental markets on productivity. Evidence from across Sub-Saharan Africa suggests that rental markets contribute to equity and are beneficial to the poor and women (see chapter 3). Regarding regularization of tenure for squatters in urban slums, evidence from Argentina, Indonesia, Peru, and the Philippines points to increases in investment, while empirical investigations in Tanzania indicate that benefits from regularization would exceed costs if cost-effective approaches of regularization were used (see chapter 3). Regarding the benefits of scaling up for gender equity, evidence suggests that improving women's access to productive resources such as fertilizer and land increases their productivity by 10 to 30 percent; given that more than 70 percent of farming activities in Africa are undertaken by women farmers, increasing their access to land, as was done in Ethiopia and Rwanda, would invariably increase agricultural productivity and food security (see chapter 3).

Conflict Prevention and Management to Generate Peace Dividends

Scaling up measures to prevent and manage conflict would generate considerable benefits for peace and social cohesion. Land is at the center of varying types of conflicts, including conflicts with colonial or other historical roots, such as dispossession of local people and subsequent claims for restitution in Kenya, Liberia, Sierra Leone, and Southern Africa; ethnic conflicts associated with rising population densities, as in Burundi and Rwanda; conflicts involving the return of internally displaced people, as in South Sudan and Uganda; and farmer-herder conflicts over land, as in Kenya, Nigeria, and Tanzania. The most relevant elements of the scaling-up program are resolving land disputes, managing expropriations, and developing postconflict land administration. These are essential for generating peace dividends and social cohesion.

Environmental Management and Protection

Scaling up land use planning is essential for protecting the public interest against damage from the irrational behavior or unintended consequences of individuals exercising their property rights. For example, to protect common-property resources such as rangelands and forests, combining the recognition of individual and common property rights with proper land use planning would provide an enhanced solution to the problem. Improved land use planning is necessary to delineate and facilitate protection of environmental, cultural, and social resources; it is also important to improve infrastructure and other public services, especially in urban slums. Furthermore, improved planning would enable the sustainable exploitation of natural resources, including agricultural land, forests, water, and minerals.

Decentralized Governance and Sustainable Land Administration

Scaling up the modernization of systems, especially property valuation and land information systems as well as land tax policies, would provide benefits by generating land-related revenue, as demonstrated in East Asian countries and

Ghana (see chapter 6). This increase in revenues is necessary to fund local government programs and the operational costs of land administration, essential for promoting decentralized governance and sustainability of land administration.

Comparing the Benefits to the Costs of the Scaling-Up Program

While lack of data and difficulties in quantifying benefits do not allow estimation of an aggregate figure against which to compare the costs of the scaling-up program (US$4.50 billion), the qualitative assessment of the benefits undertaken in this book, together with the documentation from case studies, leaves no doubt that the expected benefits of the scaling-up program would exceed the costs. The scaling-up program is critical to ensure that African countries achieve shared and sustained growth above the 5 percent achieved in the last decade.

Notes

1. The estimated registration costs are based on unit costs of US$500–US$1,000 per village or community in Tanzania and US$2,000–US$10,000 per community in Mozambique.
2. Botswana, the Comoros, Equatorial Guinea, Mali, Mauritius, Rwanda, South Africa, Sudan, and Swaziland.

References

African Union. 2009. "Declaration on Land Issues and Challenges in Africa." Assembly/AU/Decl.I (XIII) Rev.1, African Union, Addis Ababa, July.

African Union, UN (United Nations) Economic Commission for Africa, and African Development Bank. n.d. "Draft Elements of a Five-Year LPI Strategic Plan and Roadmap (2012–2016)." African Union, Addis Ababa.

Alden Wily, L. 2003. "Community-Based Land Tenure Management: Questions and Answers about Tanzania's New Village Land Act, 1999." IIED Issues Paper 120, International Institute for Development, London.

Ali, D., K. Deininger, and M. Goldstein. 2011. "Environmental and Gender Impacts of Land Tenure Regularization in Africa: Pilot Evidence from Rwanda." Policy Research Working Paper 5765, World Bank, Washington, DC.

Brits, A. M., C. Grant, and T. Burns. 2002. "Comparative Study of Land Administration Systems with Special Reference to Thailand, Indonesia, and Karnataka (India)." Paper presented at the Regional Land Workshop, World Bank, Phnom Penh, June 4–6.

Deininger, K., D. A. Ali, and T. Alemu. 2011. "Productivity Effects of Land Rental Markets in Ethiopia: Evidence from a Matched Tenant-Landlord Sample." Policy Research Working Paper 5727, World Bank, Washington, DC.

Deininger, K., D. A. Ali, S. Holden, and J. Zevenbergen. 2007. "Rural Land Certification in Ethiopia: Process, Initial Impact, and Implications for Other African Countries." Policy Research Working Paper 4218, World Bank, Washington, DC.

Deininger, K., H. Selod, and A. Burns. 2012. "The Land Governance Assessment Framework: Identifying and Monitoring Good Practice in the Land Sector." World Bank, Washington, DC.

Government of Uganda. 2001. "Land Sector Strategic Plan 2001–2011." Ministry of Lands, Water, and Environment, Kampala.

Rukuni, M., J. M. Nyoni, and E. Sithole. 2009. "Policy Options for Optimization of the Use of Land for Agricultural Productivity and Production in Zimbabwe." Third draft report submitted to the Agrarian Sector Technical Review Group and World Bank, Washington, DC.

United Republic of Kenya. 2009. "Sessional Paper No. 3 of 2009 on National Land Policy, August 2009." Government Printer for the Ministry of Lands, Nairobi.

United Republic of Tanzania. 2005. "Strategic Plan for Implementation of the Land Laws 2005/6–2014/5." Ministry of Lands, Housing, and Human Settlement Development, Dar es Salaam, April.

USAID (U.S. Agency for International Development). 2009–10. "Kenyan Civil Society Strengthening Program: Summary of Sub-Grants/Implementing Partners." USAID, Washington, DC, October 2009–September 2010.

Warnest, M., and K. C. Bell. 2009. "Country Focus Philippines." Presentation at the ICT and Rural Access Workshop, Sustainable Development Network Week, World Bank, Washington, DC, February 26.

World Bank. 2004. "Zimbabwe Land Reform Support Project." Project Completion Note, World Bank, Washington, DC.

———. 2007. *World Development Report 2008: Agriculture for Development.* Washington, DC: World Bank.

———. 2011. *Doing Business 2012: Doing Business in a More Transparent World.* Washington, DC: World Bank.

Glossary

This glossary compiles definitions from a variety of sources. The definitions are not tied to any jurisdiction and therefore are not necessarily technically correct in any particular jurisdiction. But they should provide a basic understanding on which the reader can seek more clarity and articulation. An important source is Williamson et al. (2010), which had extracted them from the following sources: the United Nations Economic Commission for Europe, Working Party on Land Administration glossary; the Bathurst Declaration glossary; and the Land Tenure Lexicon: Glossary of Terms from English- and French-Speaking West Africa. Additional sources include the Economist glossary; the UNAVCO glossary, which is a useful source for definitions in geodetic surveying; and the U.K. Ordnance Survey glossary.[1]

A

Accuracy. The closeness of the results of observations, computations, or estimates to the true values or the values accepted as being true. Accuracy relates to the exactness of the operation by which the result is obtained.

Adjudication. A process whereby the ownership of and rights to land are officially determined.

Aerial photograph. A photograph taken by a camera mounted onto some form of flying object within the Earth's atmosphere. The resultant images are used in geographic information systems (GISs) as a background layer or by surveyors to digitize.

Africa geodetic reference framework (AFREF). An African initiative with international support designed to unify the coordinate reference systems in Africa using global navigation satellite systems and, in particular, the global positioning system as the primary positioning tool.

African Doppler Survey. A multinational effort to establish primary control (via Doppler satellite observations) on the African continent. The four computing centers use three different point-positioning programs: DOPL79, GEODOP V, and ORB-SPP.

Alternative dispute resolution. Any method of resolving disputes other than by litigation.

Analog. Continuously variable signals or data.

Assessment. A determination of the tax level of a property based on its relative market value.

B

Base mapping. Usually associated with topographic mapping covering a country or region at different scales.

Basic scale. The scale at which a survey is undertaken. For U.K. Ordnance Survey mapping, three scales (1:1,250, urban; 1:2,500, urban and rural; 1:10,000, mountain and moorland) are used.

Boundary. Either the physical objects marking the limits of a property or an imaginary line or surface marking the division between two legal estates. Boundary is also used to describe the division between features with different administrative, legal, land use, and topographic characteristics.

Build, own, operate, and transfer (BOOT). A management term referring to development projects in which the contracts between the landowner (usually the government) and the developer include arrangements for building, owning, operating, and transferring the assets. BOOT contracts are popular with countries that need to develop basic infrastructure, such as roads, electricity grids, industrial estates, and so on.

C

Cadastral index map. A map showing the legal property framework of all land within an area, including property boundaries, administrative boundaries, parcel identifiers and sometimes the estimated area of each parcel, road reserves, and administrative names.

Cadastral map. An official map showing the boundaries of land parcels, including the buildings on land, the parcel identifier, and sometimes references to boundary corner monumentation. Cadastral maps may also show limited topographic features.

Cadastral mapping. The process of producing a cadastral map, usually as a result of cadastral surveying.

Cadastral surveying. The surveying and documenting of land parcel boundaries in support of a country's land administration or land registration system. The survey often results in a cadastral survey plan that may or may not be used to create or update a cadastral map.

Cadastre. A register of land information. According to the International Federation of Surveyors definition, a cadastre is normally a parcel-based and up-to-date land information system containing a record of interests in land (that is, rights, restrictions, and responsibilities).

Capacity. The ability of individuals and organizations or organizational units to perform functions effectively, efficiently, and sustainably.

Capacity building. The creation of an enabling environment with appropriate policy and legal frameworks, institutional development, including community participation, human resources development, and strengthening of managerial systems in a long-term, continuing process, in which all stakeholders participate. It is a comprehensive methodology aimed at providing sustainable outcomes through assessing and addressing a wide range of relevant issues and their interrelationships.

Capacity development. The process by which individuals, groups, organizations, institutions, and societies increase their abilities to perform core functions, solve problems, define and achieve objectives, and understand and deal with their development needs in a broader context and in a sustainable manner.

Cartography. The organization and communication of geographically related information in either graphic or digital form. It can include all stages from data acquisition to presentation and use.

Civil law. The largest family of legal systems, based on ancient Roman law, the use of codes rather than statutes as basic legislative instruments, and inquisitorial (rather than adversarial) court systems. Concepts of ownership, mortgage, usufruct, servitude, and good faith are related to their historical sources in Roman law.

Clarke 1866. The reference ellipsoid for the NAD27 coordinate system. a = 6378206.400 m, b = 6356583.800 m, 1/f = 294.978 698 200.

Collateral. Security for a loan, additional to the principal security.

Commercial off-the-shelf software. Commercially available specialized software that is designed for specific applications and can be used with little or no modification.

Commoditization. The treatment of rights in land as marketable commodities. Sometimes, this is called commodification.

Common law. The second-largest family of legal systems. Countries using common law are associated with colonization by the British, which applied the customs and precedents of the English system to aspects of colonial management. The major features include large bodies of specific legislation (not simple, short codes), extensive jurisdiction in the courts to interpret the legislation and make new law, and the power of a decision to operate as a precedent, binding on lower courts and influencing decisions in courts at the same level. Basic property concepts of ownership, adverse possession, mortgage, covenant, easement, trust, and collateral are related to English principles.

Consolidation. The amalgamation of land parcels into units of a different size, shape, and location. In some jurisdictions, consolidation refers to the planning and redistribution of land into units of more economic and rational size, shape, and location.

Continuously operating reference station (CORS). Fixed GPS receiver site in continuous operation.

Conveyance. A method or a document whereby rights in land are transferred from one owner to another. The rights may be full ownership or a mortgage, charge, or lease.

Covenant. An agreement, either expressed or implied, contained in a deed that creates an obligation between parties. A covenantor gives rights to the covenantee who obtains the benefit. Some covenants operate as proprietary interests and bind people who acquire the land after the covenants were made.

Customary law. Unwritten law established by long usage. Sometimes, this law is called traditional law or indigenous law.

Customary tenure. The holding of land in accordance with customary law.

D

Datum. A known position from which all height information is relatively measured. The heights expressed for points mapped on the National Grid are expressed as a height difference in meters from a known point on the harbor wall in Newlyn, Cornwall.

Deed. A legal document evidencing legal rights and obligations. The most important deeds contain the conditions on which land is transferred, mortgaged, or leased.

Deeds registration. A system of tracking changes in ownership of land in a public registration program that involves depositing into the registry the deed (or a copy) that makes the change.

Demarcation. The marking of the boundaries of each land parcel on the ground. A term used to describe a state- or jurisdiction-wide digital cadastral map.

Differential global positioning system (GPS). A technique for reducing the error in GPS-derived positions by using additional data from a reference GPS receiver at a known position. The most common form of differential GPS involves determining the combined effects of navigation message ephemeris and satellite clock errors (including the effects of selective availability) at a reference station and transmitting pseudo-range corrections in real time to a user's receiver, which applies the corrections in the process of determining its position.

Digital map. A term used by U.K. Ordnance Survey to describe a particular tile of digital map data.

Digitizing. The process of converting analog data such as graphic maps into digital form using scaling or other graphic means.

E

Eminent domain. The right of the state to take private property for public use, in well-organized systems, on the payment of just compensation to the property owner. In civil law, eminent domain is not used. The principle is referred to as expropriation and can only be done when warranted by the public interest.

Encroachment. An unauthorized intrusion on the land of another.

Encumbrance. A right to or an interest in land that belongs to someone other than the person having the benefit of the right or interest, which represents a burden on the land. The encumbrance will not prevent a transfer of title by the owner of the land, but may reduce its value.

Expropriation. The compulsory depriving of an owner of property, in systems that apply the rule of law, in return for compensation.

F

Fixed boundary. The legal boundary of a property where the precise line has been agreed and recorded. It is usually evidenced or described mathematically.

Fraud. A deliberate misstatement made to influence another to act. A fraudulent statement gives the person affected a right to set aside the contract.

Freehold. A free tenure, distinct from leasehold, in which the owner has the maximum rights permissible within the tenure system for indefinite duration.

Free and open-source software (F/OSS, FOSS) or free/libre/open-source software (FLOSS). Software that is both free and open source. It is liberally licensed and its source code is available so that grant users can use, copy, study, change, and improve its design.

Fundamental station. A core geodetic ground station with at least one geodetic very-long-baseline interferometry (VLBI) telescope (ideally two), a satellite laser ranging (SLR) station (with some stations having lunar laser ranging capability), at least three GNSS/GPS stations to provide local tie information and monitor site deformation, a DORIS beacon, terrestrial survey instruments to determine and monitor local ties to the millimeter level, a superconducting or, preferably, an absolute gravimeter, meteorological sensors, and a variety of other sensors such as seismometers, tiltmeters, and water vapor radiometers.

G

General boundary. A legal boundary of a property where the precise line on the ground has not been determined. A general boundary is usually evidenced by physical monuments.

Geodetic network. A scientifically measured network of monuments laid over the Earth's surface identified by surveying equipment or by satellite geodesy.

Geodetic reference frames. The basis for three-dimensional, time-dependent positioning in global, regional, and national geodetic networks, for spatial applications such as the cadastre, engineering construction, precise navigation, geo-information acquisition, geo-dynamics, sea level, and other geo-scientific studies.

Geographic information. Information about objects or phenomena that are associated with a location relative to the surface of the Earth. A special case of spatial information.

Geographic information system (GIS). A system for capturing, storing, checking, integrating, analyzing, and displaying data about the Earth that is spatially referenced. It is normally taken to include a spatially referenced database and appropriate applications software.

Global navigational satellite system (GNSS). General term for a positioning system like GPS, GLONASS (global navigation satellite system), Galileo, and COMPASS.

Global positioning system (GPS). A satellite-based navigation and positioning system that enables horizontal and vertical positions to be determined; it is a GNSS maintained and operated by the United States.

Gross domestic product. A measure of economic activity in a country. It is calculated by adding the total value of a country's annual output of goods and services.

I

Internal rate of return. The average annual return generated by an investment over a specific number of years from the time the investment is made. It is a component of an investment's net present value and accounts for an investment's net cash flow, which is the difference between its projected revenues less its projected costs, or expenses.

International GNSS Service (IGS). Formerly the International GPS Service, a voluntary federation of more than 200 worldwide agencies that pool resources and permanent GPS and GLONASS station data to generate precise GPS and GLONASS products. The IGS is committed to providing the highest-quality data and products as the standard for

GNSSs in support of Earth science research, multidisciplinary applications, and education. The IGS includes two GNSSs—GPS and the Russian GLONASS—and intends to incorporate future GNSSs. The IGS is the highest-precision international civilian GPS community.

International terrestrial reference frame (ITRF). The most accurate global reference frame for scientific and other applications.

International terrestrial reference system. A world spatial reference system co-rotating with the Earth in its diurnal motion in space.

Investment appraisal. A technique used to determine whether an investment is likely to be profitable.

L

Land. In most systems of law, the surface of the Earth, the materials beneath, the air above, and all things fixed to the soil. Notable exceptions are found in communist countries and in countries, such as Indonesia, where land is controlled by the nation.

Land administration. The processes run by government using public or private sector agencies related to land tenure, land value, land use, and land development.

Land administration projects. Projects to build, reengineer, or improve land administration systems. They include institutionalization of land administration systems capable of both reflecting and improving existing people-to-land relationships as the focus of many international aid and antipoverty initiatives.

Land administration system. An infrastructure for implementing land policies and land management strategies in support of sustainable development. The infrastructure includes institutional arrangements, a legal framework, processes, standards, land information, management and dissemination systems, and technologies required to support allocation, land markets, valuation, control of use, and development of interests in land.

Land governance. The activities associated with determining and implementing sustainable land policies.

Land information system. A system for acquiring, processing, storing, and distributing information about land.

Land management. The activities associated with the management of land as a resource to achieve sustainable social, environmental, and economic development.

Land reform. The various processes involved in altering the pattern of land tenure and land use of a specified area. Some of the processes involve land administration, but most of the processes are intensely political.

Land register. A register, usually public, used to record the existence of deeds or title documents, thereby protecting rights in land and facilitating the transfer of those rights.

Land registration. The process of recording rights in land through either the registration of deeds or the registration of title to land, so that any person acquiring a property in good faith can trust the information published by the registry. Land registration programs range from well-run, deeds-based registration systems, which virtually guarantee title, to Torrens-style systems, which guarantee title. Title registration is positive in nature and confers and protects the title. It is different from deeds registration, which provides a degree of confidence through registration but does not positively confer title.

Land tenure. The manner of holding rights in and occupying land.

Land tenure regularization. A deliberate process aimed at bringing informal and unauthorized settlements within the official, legal, and administrative systems of land management.

Land title. Evidence of a person's rights to or ownership of land (the deeds or certificate of ownership) or the ownership itself, depending on the context.

Land transfer. The transfer of rights in land.

Land use. The manner in which land is used.

Land value. The worth of a property, determined by one of a variety of ways, each of which can give rise to a specific estimate.

Large-scale base map. A map showing certain fundamental information, used as a base on which additional data of specialized nature are compiled or overprinted and usually with a scale of 1:10,000 or greater in rural areas or 1:2,500 or greater in urban areas.

Laser-induced direction and range (LIDAR). Airborne laser scanning system that accurately measures Digital Elevation Models (DEMs). It may be used to monitor and predict floods, detect buildings, measure the height of buildings and trees, and produce general DEMs.

Leasehold. The property right created by a lease, which is a contract by a landlord (the lessor) giving exclusive possession to a tenant (the lessee) for an agreed amount of money for an agreed period of time.

M

Market value. The most probable sales price of a real estate property in terms of money, assuming a competitive and open market.

Metadata. A structured summary of information that describes the data (data about data).

Mortgage. An interest in land created by a written instrument providing security for the mortgagee (the lender) for performance of a duty or the payment of a debt by the mortgagor (the borrower). In some legal systems, the mortgagee has the power to sell or forfeit the property when interest is not paid in time or the loan is not paid off in accordance with the contract.

N

Net present value (NPV). A measure used to decide whether or not to proceed with an investment. Net means that both the costs and benefits of the investment are included. To calculate NPV, first add together all the expected benefits from the investment, now and in the future, then add together all the expected costs, then work out what these future benefits and costs are worth now by adjusting future cash flow using an appropriate discount rate, and then subtract the costs from the benefits. If the NPV is negative, then the investment cannot be justified by the expected returns. If the NPV is positive, it can, although it pays to compare it with the NPVs of alternative investment opportunities before proceeding.

O

Orthophoto. Photographic image, rectified to remove the distortions caused by variations in terrain height, resulting in an image in which all pixels are to the same scale.

Ownership. The most comprehensive right a person can have with respect to a thing (in this context, land). Full ownership usually includes the exclusive right to use and dispose of the thing (land), but the exact rights vary from country to country.

P

Parcel. An area of land with defined boundaries, under unique ownership for specific real property rights.

Pixel. A picture element of a raster image as displayed on a screen or raster plot.

Plot. An area of land identifiable on a map.

Point. A zero-dimensional spatial abstraction of an object represented by a coordinate pair.

Policy. The stated goals for determining how land should be used, managed, and conserved in order to meet social, environmental, and economic objectives.

Precision. A measure of the repeatability of a measurement. In the context of this report, precision quantifies the ability to repeat the determination of a position within a reference frame (internal precision) and can be measured using various statistical methods on samples of estimated positions. Although precision does not imply accuracy, high precision is a prerequisite for consistently high accuracy and is necessary to resolve changes in position over time. The precision of a reference frame itself (external precision) refers to the variation in the reference frame parameters (origin, orientation, and scale) that arise from statistical variation in the data used to define the frame.

Property appraisal. An estimation of the market value of real property.

R

Reference frame. A set of three-dimensional Cartesian coordinates (x, y, z), and the rates of change of these coordinates over time, for a network of points on the Earth's surface that defines the coordinates for other sites.

Reference system. The theories, models, and physical constants underlying a reference frame.

Remote sensing. The process of obtaining information about an object while separated by some distance from the subject. Practically, this term describes the process of using sensors mounted on satellites to observe the Earth's geology, surface, and atmosphere.

Resolution. A measure of the ability to detect quantities. High resolution implies a high degree of discrimination but does not imply accuracy. For example, in a collection of data in which the coordinates are rounded to the nearest meter, resolution will be 1 meter, but the accuracy may be +/− 5 meters or worse.

S

Satellite imagery. Photographs of Earth or other planets made by means of artificial satellites.

Scanning. Capturing an image using an optical input device that uses light-sensing equipment. The image is translated into a digital signal that can be manipulated by optical character recognition software or graphics software.

Security. An interest in an asset given to secure repayment of a debt.

Security of tenure. At the most basic level, when "other people believe the land you occupy and use is the land that you are allowed to live on and use" (UN-Habitat 2004, 13). Legal security exists insofar as the law of a country protects the continuing use.

Social Tenure Domain Model (STDM). A pro-poor land administration support tool aimed at improving tenure security of the poor and vulnerable groups like women. It is meant specifically for countries with very little cadastral coverage in urban areas with slums or in rural areas under customary rule. The focus of STDM is on all relationships between people and land, independent of the level of formalization or legality of those relationships.

Spatial data or information. Data or information relating to the land, sea, or air that can be referenced to a position on the Earth's surface. It is also the key to planning, sustainable management, and development of natural resources at the local, national, regional, and global level.

Spatial data infrastructure (SDI). A term that describes the fundamental spatial data sets, the standards that enable them to be integrated, the distribution network that provides access to them, the policies and administrative principles that ensure compatibility among jurisdictions and agencies, and the people, including users, providers, and value adders, who are interested at a certain level, starting at the local level and proceeding through the state, national, and regional levels to the global level. The SDI concept is developed at these levels.

Sporadic registration. A method of bringing land into a registration program through ad hoc methods, usually on transfer of the land.

Squatter. A person who uses land without title. Many countries are unable to provide titles to citizens who are inevitably squatters, especially those who live in urban slums. Here, imperatives of housing and livelihood demand that even squatters be protected against arbitrary eviction.

Subdivision. The process of dividing a land parcel into smaller parcels.

Sustainable development. Development that meets the needs of the present without compromising the ability of future generations to meet their own needs. The field of sustainable development can be conceptually broken into three parts: environmental sustainability, economic sustainability, and sociopolitical sustainability.

Systematic registration. A method of bringing all parcels of land in a defined region into the system through a single process of public education, adjudication of titles, surveying or other means of identifying the parcels, creation of unique parcel numbers, and issuance of titles.

T

Temporary reference station. A temporary CORS.

Tenure. The way in which the rights, restrictions, and responsibilities that people have with respect to the land are held. The cadastre may record different forms of land tenure such as ownership, leasehold, and different types of common, communal, or customary land tenure.

Transfer. Either the act by which title to property is conveyed from one person to another or the document used to pass registered land to the transferee.

Trust. In common law, an arrangement by which legal title to property is held by one person on behalf of and for the benefit of another.

Trustee. An entity that holds a trust.

W

World Geodetic System 1984 (WGS-84). The latest version of the Department of Defense World Geodetic System, which is consistent with ITRF at the centimeter level (but is less accurate than the ITRF).

Note

1. For the United Nations Economic Commission for Europe, Working Party on Land Administration glossary, http://www.unece.org/hlm/wpla/publications/laglossary .html; for the Bathurst Declaration glossary, http://www.fig.net/pub/figpub/pub21/ figpub21.htm; for the Land Tenure Lexicon: Glossary of Terms from English- and French-Speaking West Africa, http://www.iied.org/pubs/pdfs/7411IIED.pdf; for the Economist glossary, http://www.economist.com/economics-a-to-z; for the UNAVCO glossary, http://facility.unavco.org/data/glossary.html#d; and for the U.K. Ordnance Survey glossary, http://www.ordnancesurvey.co.uk/oswebsite/ aboutus/reports/misc/glossary.html.

References

United Nations Habitat (UN-Habitat). 2004. *Pro-Poor Land Management: Integrating Slums into City Planning Approaches*. Nairobi: United Nations.

Williamson, I., S. Enemark, J. Wallace, and A. Rajabffard. 2010. *Land Administration for Sustainable Development*. Redlands, CA: ESRI Press Academic.

Index

Boxes, figures, notes, and tables are indicated by *b*, *f*, *n*, and *t*, respectively.